onyourown.com

e-mail messages to my daughter

onyourown.com

e-mail messages to my daughter

Bruce & Stan

PROMISE PRESS

An Imprint of Barbour Publishing

Published by Promise Press, an imprint of Barbour Publishing, Inc., P.O. Box 719, Uhrichsville, Ohio 44683, http://www.barbourbooks.com

Member of the
Evangelical Christian
Publishers Association

Printed in the United States of America.

CONTENTS

Lessons About Your Life

Lessons About Your God

Introduction

Our families met each other almost twenty years ago, and we've been best friends ever since. From the beginning we found that we had a lot in common: we have daughters the same age, sons the same age, and dogs the same age. Our kids have gone through school as best friends (but the dogs haven't been too compatible). Over the years, the Bickel and Jantz families have shared several vacations and lots of laughs. Most importantly, our friendship has been strongly bonded by our shared beliefs.

Recently our daughters each went away to college (Lindsey Bickel to Westmont College and Hillary Jantz to Biola University). One evening we were talking about the experience of having your little girl leave home for the first time. We found that our feelings were similar (every dad has them), and we discovered something interesting about the way each of us was communicating to our daughter. We were sending e-mail messages.

Now that doesn't sound too personal, but it's the reality of life (and we suppose technology) these days. At first we thought it was a little strange sending these electronic mail messages rather than calling or writing letters. They seemed cold and, well, *digital*. But each of us warmed up to the idea and soon found that e-mail was the perfect way to talk about any topic we could think of (and believe us, we could think of plenty).

And here's the best part: The girls loved it. They enjoyed hearing from their dads, and it was no big deal to click on the "Reply" button and answer back. Honestly, that's the beauty of e-mail. Imagine writing a letter to someone you love and getting a response the same day. It just doesn't happen. But with e-mail you hear back—sometimes only a few words— almost instantly. It's the way kids communicate with each other these days (when they're not out in a group somewhere asking for a table for sixteen at the local Denny's). And it's the way we've been telling our daughters just how much we love them.

A few months ago we decided that as long as we had our daughters' attention, we would make an attempt to say some things each of them could use as they established lives of their own. You know how it goes. There's never enough time to tell your kids the things you want them to know. Whether they're at home, away from home, or about to leave, you wish you could tell them just one more thing. Well, for us, sending these e-mail messages was the perfect way to share our hearts about the things that matter most in life.

In a way, the messages in this book are a collection of "just one more things." We actually sent them to our daughters, and they gave us valuable—and usually immediate—feedback. We hope that you can identify with these living lessons for life's journey. We hope they help you as you talk to, write, call, or even e-mail your own daughter.

A Note to the Reader

This book contains actual e-mail messages that we sent to our daughters when they went "on their own." We have edited the text only slightly, to avoid comments that might be embarrassing to them (or incriminating to us). Personal references to former boyfriends and occasional bouts with the stomach flu have been deleted because they would be of no interest to any readers of this book (except, perhaps, former boyfriends).

For purposes of this book, we gave each e-mail a title that reflects the theme of what we wrote. When originally written, the e-mails had more generic titles (like "How's it going?" "What's happening?" or "Are you still alive because I haven't heard from you in such a long time that I'm wondering whether I should stop sending tuition payments to the college?").

Don't be confused if the time sequence seems out of order. The e-mails in this book have been arranged topically, not chronologically.

Our publisher, Promise Press, intentionally did not edit these e-mails to give them an identical style. Consequently, you may notice a difference between the e-mails written by Bruce (to Lindsey) and those written by Stan (to Hillary). When we write books together, we use a compatible style. But these e-mails were not written with a book in mind, so they are our personal "dad to daughter" writing style: Stan is a born writer, so his e-mails tend to be long and eloquently written; Bruce hasn't outgrown his desire to be a stand-up humorist, so his e-mails tend to be shorter (with an occasional punch line).

A little more information may help you understand the context of these e-mails. As these e-mails were written:

> Lindsey is at Westmont College, about 250 miles away from home. She is majoring in Communications and anticipating a career in journalism. Her passions include Broadway musicals, friends, and fitness. Her weaknesses are worrying and parking tickets. Her brother, Matt, is in high school, still "stuck" at home with Mom (Cheryl), Dad (Bruce), and the dog (Sadie).

Hillary attends Biola University, also about 250 miles away from home. Her major is Graphic Design, and she is looking forward to a job in that field. She has a zest for life and enjoys people. Her brother, Scott, is in high school back at home with Mom (Karin), Dad (Stan), and the dog (Zoey).

Here is a final personal word of advice to other dads (and moms) who are at the stage of sending children "on their own." If you communicate by e-mail, then save those messages. Save the ones you write to your children, and save the ones they send to you. After a few years, your compendium of e-mails will trace your child's growth into adulthood and the growth of your relationship with each other.

Lessons About You

The LORD hates people with twisted hearts,
but he delights in those who have integrity.

Proverbs 11:20

Inbox

Subject: Integrity
From: Dad
To: Lindsey

Message: I'm glad, sort of, that you are on your own, but I sure miss you a lot. Especially at dinnertime. I miss talking about the events of the day and getting to hear your perspective. I had this great discussion last night with your mom and Matt. We talked about all that is happening in the political campaigns, particularly on the issue of integrity. You know the kind of thing: Who has it? Who doesn't? Does it matter? Because you eat your meals about 250 miles away from our dinner table, I'll fill you in on what you missed (so long as you promise to think about it the next time you are chomping food at the dining commons).

- Integrity is simply doing what you promised you would do. It is *telling* the truth and *doing* the truth.
- Integrity is doing the right thing (even if no one would know that you did the wrong thing).
- Integrity is accepting the blame when you have made a mistake (especially if you could dodge it or shift it to someone else).

People who lack integrity probably got started making ethical compromises on the small things. It is the small ones that are really tempting—the tiny breaches of integrity that hardly seem to matter: No one may know, no one may get hurt, and you will come out looking better. But don't compromise on the small things, because you will build up an immunity. Your conscience will become calloused. Then you begin to struggle with doing the right thing on the bigger issues. It is just easier to always do the right thing. Big or little. Private or public. Just do what is right.

Integrity always matters. If for no other reason, because it matters to God. But beyond that, it keeps you as the kind of person you want to live with. And that's important because you have to live with yourself your entire life.

Well, that about sums it up. See! When you are away from home you miss a lot more than your mom's cooking.

Love, Dad

It is extremely embarrassing to come to your senses
and find out you haven't any.

Subject: Common Sense
From: Dad
To: Lindsey

Message: Sorry that I missed your call last night. Mom filled me in on some of the details. Sounds like you had a real adventure. I'm glad you had lots of fun (and I'm relieved to hear that there are no teeth, toes, or eyeballs scattered over the freeway).

While I'm on the subject of you doing crazy stuff that could be a little dangerous—(do you like that smooth transition into the "fatherly advice" mode?)—let me say this: Much of what you need to learn at college will *not* come from books and professors. It happens outside the classroom and the library. It is the process of learning how to use common sense. Believe me, you will need to rely on common sense and good judgment much more in life than what you will learn in your world civilization class (assuming that you have been attending your world civ class).

I know that you have a good dose of common sense. But I worry that sometimes you are having so much fun that you forget about using it. If you were living at home, I could give you a few gentle reminders each time that you walked out the door. But since you're not here, and since I'm not living in your dorm room, here are seven simple questions you can ask yourself before you start your next "adventure." Think of this as sort of a "dad-away-from-home" checklist:

1. *Is it safe?* Here is a clue. If it involves handguns, juggling chain saws, or driving blindfolded, you may want to reconsider.
2. *Who came up with this idea?* If the person has recently been arrested, expelled, or hospitalized, you may want to spend a few additional moments in

contemplative reflection.

3. *What's the worst thing that could happen?* Think through all the possible scenarios. If any of them involve obituaries, CPR, police lineups, or calling me for money, then do it another way.

4. *How will the newspaper headline read?* If this got reported in the newspaper, how would you feel? If words like "foolish," "embarrassed," or "humiliated" come to mind, that ought to tell you something.

5. *What will your mom and dad say when they find out?* I admit it. This is the least important of all of the questions on the checklist. But just count on the fact that we will find out. You know we always do.

6. *Will this seem like a dumb thing five years from now?* A tattoo of your favorite musical group may seem like a great idea now, but a prospective employer may wonder why it says "The Blooming Onions" on your ankle.

7. *Will God be pleased with this activity?* You have always made great decisions in this area, but I want to add

this question to the list because it is so important. This doesn't mean that you can't have fun. Just the opposite. I am convinced that Jesus used to yuck it up with Peter and John and the rest of the guys as they were walking from town to town. But whether we are being serious or just goofing around, we should remember that God is involved with what we do.

Whenever you go out with the gang, you always do a good job of making sure everyone is included in the fun. So think about this. Common sense can be like a shy friend. It kind of stays in the background. Sometimes it can get lost or overlooked in all the excitement. But it is a friendship that should be developed and nurtured.

Make common sense your best friend. Take it with you wherever you go. It will be invaluable to you (and your mother and I will sleep better at night).

Love ya! Dad

P.S. At least you tell us about your scary adventures *after* they are over. It you told us before they happened, we would be calling emergency prayer meetings at church.

So make every effort to apply the benefits
of these promises to your life.

2 Peter 1:5

Subject: Effort
From: Dad
To: Hillary

Message: Your mother told me that you talked to her last night about your Spanish class, how you were struggling a bit now that the semester is winding down. As you might expect, I asked Mom, "Well, how much *effort* is she putting into the class?"

Since you were a little girl, I can remember encouraging you to put a little effort into everything you do. Now as I look back—and even as I think about your Spanish class—I wonder if I've been asking the right question and encouraging you in the right way. You see, *effort* is the same as *trying hard*. It's using your energy and strength to do something, whether you're trying to lift something (which really doesn't apply to you) or get something done (like getting a good grade in Spanish).

I don't doubt for one minute that you have put effort into the important stuff in your life. You may not *appear* on the outside to be trying hard, because by your nature you are a very relaxed person. But I know that when it counts, you will muster the energy and put in the time to get done what it is you need to get done (although, like me, you'll sometimes wait until the last minute). So, I don't worry that you will make every effort to do well in Spanish, even though it's not your favorite subject.

When you think about it, it's almost mandatory to put effort into your schoolwork, because you know that you're going to receive a grade. You're going to get a reward—or fail to get a reward. The same thing goes for athletics, or a performance of any kind, for that matter. You make an effort because you are promised a reward if you do well.

But what if the reward—or in some cases the lack of a

reward—wasn't immediate? What if you knew that no matter how much effort you put in now, you wouldn't get a reward for several years, or maybe not at all? Would you be as motivated to give it your best, or would you have a tendency to let it slide, or perhaps not do anything? I thought about this last night, and I wanted to run an idea by you.

The idea is this: I think we have a tendency to put a great deal of effort into those things with an immediate reward—or deadline—and very often we put little or no effort into those things where the reward is so far out there that we can't even see it.

There's a great little booklet I first read when I was about your age that sums up this human tendency perfectly. It's called *The Tyranny of the Urgent*. Isn't that a great title? You really don't even have to read the booklet in order to figure out the theme (although I want you to read it—in fact I'll send you a copy). Basically, *The Tyranny of the Urgent* says that the urgent things in life will always get our attention and effort, while the things that aren't urgent will always be set aside for another day. Yet it is those *nonurgent* things that are very often the *most important.*

In my life, I've found that my relationship with God is one of those nonurgent but very important things. Sadly, when I should be making God my top priority, I often submit to the tyranny of the urgent. I put my effort into those things that scream out for my attention because there are immediate rewards if I do them and immediate consequences if I don't.

But what's more important than God? What has more value, both here and in the future, than my relationship with Him? Even though there may not be a reward *now* for the effort I put into my relationship with God, God has promised an eternal reward for those who seek Him (Jeremiah 29:11–13). Not only that, but our lives *here and now* will be much more peaceful, powerful, and pleasing to God.

I've found that a little effort helps when it comes to growing as a Christian. Spiritual progress won't happen by sticking a Bible under your pillow at night (it just gives you a stiff neck). You need to spend time in God's Word, you need to take time to pray, and you need to be around other Christians on a regular basis so you can worship Him together.

So, as you study for Spanish and put more effort into the class, think about putting more effort into your relationship with God. It will satisfy you more than you'll ever know and please God in the process.

Love, Dad

Whatever happens. . .
may the Lord give you joy.

Philippians 3:1

Subject: Enthusiasm
From: Dad
To: Hillary

Message: Things have seemed a little quiet around the house since you went back to school, and I think I've figured out why. We miss your unbridled, unabashed, unashamed *enthusiasm*. Don't get me wrong. It's not like the rest of us are moping around the house with nothing to live for. But without you around life is just a little duller because we don't have that "warp factor nine" level of enthusiasm for life you are famous for. I love that about you, and I miss it.

Having said that, I've got something very special to share with you, and it relates to enthusiasm. Most people equate enthusiasm with extreme interest or excitement, and that's not a bad way to look at it. As far as you are concerned, you get enthusiastic about things or events—whether it's a new stuffed animal, a funny movie, or a trip to Disneyland—because you're interested in them, and that creates excitement. You can't wait to see and touch that new character, laugh your way through a movie, or walk through the gates to the Magic Kingdom.

The excitement aspect of enthusiasm is great, and that certainly defines your personality. But there's another dimension to enthusiasm that gets more to the heart of what I want to say, and this also reveals a lot about you. When you break the word *enthusiasm* down, you essentially have two words: *en* and *theos*. Now it's been a while since I've taken a foreign language in school, but I think I still remember what these two words mean.

En basically means *in*, and *theos*, well, that's the word for *God*. So, in essence, to be enthusiastic means to have *God in you*. Isn't that great? Just by being enthusiastic, you are showing the world that God matters in your life.

Now I'm not saying that people who aren't enthusiastic don't have God in them. We both know that Christians can be some of the most pessimistic people around. On the other hand, people who know God personally *should* be the most enthusiastic people there are. We should be the world's greatest enthusiasts, because we have the greatest reason to be excited about life. Our future with God is bright and certain. Someday we're going to the most spectacular, *Magnificent* Kingdom ever, which should create tremendous interest and anticipation.

Well, I can't explain why Christians aren't more enthusiastic, but I thank God that you are the most enthusiastic person I know. Never get discouraged in your enthusiasm, even when others may resent it (and they will because you make them feel dull). As you finish school and do the things you've always dreamed about doing, may your enthusiasm fill your days and shine brightly for God.

Love, Dad

Just over the hill is a beautiful valley,
but you must climb the hill to see it.

Subject: Focus
From: Dad
To: Lindsey

Message: I know that you are becoming discouraged by the routine of it all. Much of what you do each day seems boring and mundane. But stay focused on the long view of things. Realize that you are working with a goal in mind. Effort now will result in privileges later.

Be willing to do today what others will not do, so you can do tomorrow what others cannot do.

Love, Dad

With the fearful strain that is on me night and day,
if I did not laugh I should die.

Abraham Lincoln

Subject: Humor

From: Dad

To: Lindsey

Message: Thanks for the note. I got it in the mail today. It cracked me up and kept a smile on my face for the rest of the day. I've taped it to my computer monitor.

Your note got me thinking. I know we don't look much alike. Your hair is blond and curly, and mine is just gray (prematurely, I might add). You've got a sporty look about you and I am more, well, sedentary in appearance. Let's face it, except for our distinctive lack of height, we don't look related. But there is a strong family resemblance between us. . .our sense of humor.

Laughter is one of our strongest family traits. I hope

you learn to use it to your advantage. It can make your life much more enjoyable. Everybody likes a person with a good sense of humor, and it can disarm people who are angry with you. A sense of humor can be destructive, however, if you are not careful.

Let me give you three simple rules for laughter and humor:

Laugh at *yourself.* This will always be the greatest source of humor (particularly for you). Don't ever take yourself so seriously that you can't find humor in the things you say and do. Of course it will be easy to laugh at yourself when you do something goofy (like your frequent giggling attacks when you're drinking, which cause you to spew your drink out your nose).

Laugh with *others.* Some people can't (or won't) see the humor in their situations. Other people may not be as comfortable with their goof-ups as you are with yours. Make sure they are laughing before you get started. If they start, then join in; if they don't, then suppress your laughter (but be careful not to blow out your eardrums).

Laugh often. Laughter is good for your health. It releases tension and stress. It has physical and mental benefits. How do you think that George Burns got to be so old?

You will find that laughter removes all barriers. When people are laughing together, there is no young and old, no boss or subordinate. It is just people enjoying their existence.

A sense of humor is a valuable asset. Appreciate it in yourself and in others. I'm serious about this. It is no laughing matter.

Love, Dad

Creativity is not dulled by age, only by disuse.

O. Aldrich Wakeford

Subject: Creativity

From: Dad

To: Lindsey

Message: I don't know why, but for some reason I was wide awake this morning at about 12:30 A.M. thinking about your class schedule. Being unable to fall back to sleep, I then began thinking about your major (and your minor), your career and occupation, etc.

Are you ready for a profound tidbit of unsolicited advice? No?! Well, here it comes anyway: Creativity and imagination are more valuable than knowledge.

Think about it. Knowledge can be acquired. It can be looked up in a book. But creativity and imagination are innate. A person either has them, or not. Most people don't; you do.

This is not to say that you should abandon all pursuits of knowledge. Don't burn your textbooks, don't quit school, and don't spend all day in a yoga trance. In other words, keep doing your homework and pursue knowledge. Knowledge is the canvas on which you paint with your imagination and creativity. One has to have knowledge or else creativity and imagination have no context.

My point is this: From an employer's perspective, people with knowledge are as common as commercials during a Super Bowl telecast. But people with creativity and imagination are a rare and valuable commodity.

Since God has given you so much of what is so rare, plan to make good use of it. Look for an occupation or career where you can put your creativity and imagination to your fullest advantage and enjoyment. But since that career will no doubt require at least a modicum of knowledge, don't take any of your valuable time to daydream about your future career. Instead, why don't you just keep studying for your courses?

Remember, a future employer is going to look at your resume. Creativity and imagination won't do you much good if your GPA is in negative numbers.

Love, Dad

P.S. While you're busy studying, I'll be in charge of day-dreaming for your career. It is what I do best when I can't get to sleep at night.

Great works are performed not by strength
but by perseverance.

Samuel Johnson

Subject: Perseverance
From: Dad
To: Hillary

Message: You're getting to the point in your life when perseverance is going to become a growing factor in your success. I don't know why I'm thinking about this right now, and I'm not really sure how it applies to you right now. But I know that perseverance and persistence, when applied to any task or any goal, is going to eventually be more important to you than your talent or personality.

Here's how it works. When you were at home, we cared for you pretty much twenty-four hours a day, and we loved every minute of it! Well, maybe there were some times when your mother and I got a little frustrated with you, but honestly it's the great times we recall. And we're going to continue to have great times together as we get together for special occasions—or just for no reason at all—in the years ahead.

Because your life was more or less sheltered, you didn't need to "stick it out" too many times in order to get something done. There weren't many occasions when you had to persevere through overwhelming obstacles in order to reach a goal you had set for yourself. That didn't make you better than other kids your age who had to persist at something if they were to get anywhere at all. It just meant that when you left home to attend college, you were a little "soft" around the edges when it came to dealing with the reality of life, which isn't always easy.

Even though you're on your own to a greater degree than you've ever been before—and moving in the direction of being *completely* on your own in a couple of years—you haven't yet had to persevere through a difficult circumstance. You haven't had to discipline yourself over a long period of time (we're talking years) in order to accomplish a worthwhile goal. But that time is coming.

I'm not trying to scare you or tell you that so far your life has been easy, and now it's going to get really hard. None of us knows what the future holds. In all likelihood—and we are praying for this every day—you will have a happy life full of the usual joys and sorrows that come to any of us in the course of a lifetime. But along with the adventure of living life on your own will come the times when you'll need to draw upon an inner resolve and pray like you've never prayed before so you can get through whatever valley God is allowing you to go through.

Or you may set a goal for yourself that is so far out there and so incredible, that the only way you will accomplish it is by never giving up, which is what perseverance is all about. The great English writer Samuel Johnson said, "Great works are performed not by strength but by perseverance." William Wilberforce, who worked his entire life for the abolition of slavery in England, said:

"Our motto must continue to be *perseverance*. And ultimately I trust the Almighty will crown our efforts with success."

God did honor Wilberforce's perseverance, by the way, and slavery was eventually abolished in England, but not until *after* Wilberforce had died.

That brings up another aspect of perseverance that's very important. Just because you stick with your goal in order to get the job done, just because you tough it out during a dark time in your life, doesn't guarantee that you'll reach your goal or defeat the darkness as soon as you would like. Sometimes it will seem like the challenge will never end. But that's just the time you need to continue steadily doing what is right. Because eventually there will be a reward, and God will crown your effort with success.

There's a great verse in the Bible that talks about this. The apostle Paul wrote:

I don't mean to say that I have already achieved these things or that I have already reached perfection! But I keep working toward that day when I will finally be all that Christ Jesus saved me for and wants me to be.

(Philippians 3:12)

Honey, that's our prayer for you. More than anything else we want you to be all that Jesus wants you to be. And that's not going to happen if you simply "let it happen." It's going to take faith, hard work, and a whole lot of perseverance.

Love, Dad

The human body, with proper care,
will last a lifetime.

Subject: Health
From: Dad
To: Lindsey

Message: Sorry to hear that you aren't getting much sleep. I know it must be difficult learning to live in a dorm, adjusting to a roommate, and balancing all of the fun and responsibility of being on your own. Let me suggest that there is something else that you have to learn now that you are on your own.

Until now, you always had your mom and me to worry about your health. We'll still worry, but there is not much that we can do about it long-distance. For the most part, your health is up to you. So, don't neglect it.

Your health, good or bad, will affect everything you

do. It impacts your studies, your recreation, and your social life. If you are feeling great, then all of those things will be better. If you're feeling lousy, then everything you do will seem that way, too.

Eating healthy and getting exercise are too obvious to mention, so I won't. (Oops, I just did.) Anyway, since you don't put anything on your plate that ever had a face, and because you are jogging about seven miles a day, I'm not too worried about your diet or exercise program.

But what about sleep?! Getting enough sleep is probably the most important part of staying healthy. I can hear you scoffing, but I can prove it. Suppose you doze off in class because you aren't getting enough sleep at night. Your head will snap forward, and your skull will crack open when it hits the desk. Low cholesterol and a good pulse rate will be pretty meaningless when the contents of your cranium are spilling all over the floor. Your grades will suffer because you don't have a brain, and that missing chunk of your skull will repulse all your friends. You'll flunk out of school; you'll be friendless and penniless. You'll have to move back home with Mom and me. All because you didn't get enough sleep!

What's the moral of this e-mail? Get some sleep! (If not for yourself, do it for me. I don't want to stay awake at night worrying about whether you are getting enough sleep.)

Love, Dad

We increase our ability, stability, and responsibility when we increase our sense of accountability to God.

Subject: Responsibility
From: Dad
To: Lindsey

Message: I appreciate you hanging in there. I know things are tough, and it would be easy for you to bail out. No one would blame you if you quit. Except maybe yourself.

There is a big difference between authority and responsibility. Authority usually refers to your power over people. Responsibility usually refers to your pledge to people. Those interested only in authority usually lose it. Those willing to assume responsibility usually get it. Most people crave authority and avoid responsibility.

You've got a great sense of responsibility. I applaud it. I admire it. I envy it.

Love, Dad

Some people dream of worthy accomplishments.
Other people wake up and work hard to achieve them.
The difference is initiative.

Inbox

Subject: Initiative
From: Dad
To: Lindsey

Message: With only a week of college experience, I know you have many things to be thinking about: how much studying will be necessary; how to establish friendships; what pranks to play on the guys living on the second floor of the dorm; whether you can avoid washing any clothes until you come home at Thanksgiving. I know these questions are of cosmic significance, and I don't mean to distract you from pondering them.

However, it occurs to me that you might have a few idle moments as you walk around the campus. May I be so presumptuous as to suggest a topic worthy of your consideration and meditation at such intervals? I suggest that you contemplate "initiative."

Initiative is more than the act of doing something that needs to be done. Initiative prompts you to tackle the task before you are told, before you are asked, and before the last minute.

For example, *good* employees do what they are asked to do. *Great* employees see what needs to be done and do it before they are asked. Initiative makes the difference. Similarly, initiative can make a person a better student, friend, spouse, or parent.

You see, initiative solves the hardest part of every project: getting started. Remember that famous slogan, "Just Do It"? Well, with the tasks, projects, and responsibilities of life, that motto is applied differently depending on one's character:

The sluggard says: "I'll do it later."

The average person says: "I'll do it before it's due."

The person with initiative says: "I'll do it now."

How do you know whether you have initiative or not?

Here's an easy test: How do you feel about your alarm clock? Is it your friend or your enemy? The person with initiative wants to: get up; go out; and work on. Without initiative, it's simply: lay down; stay in; and goof off.

Now, just in case you think I am trying to make you feel guilty about having a fun time instead of doing your homework, I'm not. You've always been a hard worker. I'm just trying to give you a little encouragement to keep at it. Now that you're on your own, there will be lots of temptations to slack off or to get distracted. Hang in there, kid.

Love, Dad

P.S. I realize that you might be working so hard that you don't have time to meditate on the subject of initiative. If that's the case, then print this e-mail and give it to a friend who needs it. I would hate this great fatherly advice to go unused.

Nothing in the world can take the place of persistence.
Talent will not; nothing is more common than unsuccessful
men with talent. Genius will not; unrewarded genius is
almost a proverb. Education will not; the world is full of
educated derelicts. Persistence and determination alone
are omnipotent. The slogan "Press On" has solved,
and will solve, the problems of the human race.

Calvin Coolidge

Subject: Diligence
From: Dad
To: Lindsey

Message: Here are Five Steps to Achieve Mediocrity:

1. Only do the minimum that is required.
2. Wait until the last minute.
3. Be unprepared.
4. Accept mistakes and errors as a fact of life.
5. Let someone else do it.

Your diligence will set you apart from those who find mediocrity acceptable. Hang in there.

Love, Dad

Failure is the path of least persistence.

Inbox

Subject: Commitment
From: Dad
To: Lindsey

Message: I know you are spending a lot of time studying for your finals, so I'll keep this short. Stay committed to your long-range goal. You can get discouraged if you're only looking at the daily grind. Always remember *why* you are working so hard. Your hard study will lead to good grades. . .the good grades will lead to a great job. . . that job will lead to being queen of the world! Now, how can you risk jeopardizing that?

What you are doing today is definitely going to affect your tomorrow. Hang in there!

Love, Dad

("Queen Lindsey." It has a nice ring to it.)

Lessons About
Your Relationships

There are "friends" who destroy each other,
but a real friend sticks closer than a brother.

Proverbs 18:24

Subject: Friendship
From: Dad
To: Lindsey

Message: I just read your last e-mail. I will be praying that you establish some meaningful friendships soon. But remember that you have only been at college for three weeks. Give God a little time to direct you to the friends He wants you to have. After all, some of the friendships you establish now will probably last for your lifetime. From the perspective of sixty years or so, another few weeks shouldn't be too long to wait.

Maybe now is the right time to tell you what I was surprised to learn when I went away to college. (Yes, they had colleges in the Dark Ages—except there were no history classes because not that much had happened yet.) I suspect that you are going to discover the same thing.

Many of the friendships which I had in high school faded rather quickly. I had a group of friends, and we were pretty close. When some of us went away to college, we were sure that we would all get back together on holidays and in the summers. We did for a few times, but it wasn't the same. After a while, we lost track of each other. I still enjoy linking up with some of them from time to time. There are always some initial jokes about failing eyesight, expanding waistlines, and the hair that grows in our ears. But after that, we don't seem to have too much in common.

Please excuse that short excursion down memory lane. What I am trying to say is this: You will have much more in common with your best friends than just past memories. I know you have great friendships from high school. I think all of those kids are great (with a few notable exceptions). You will always have fun getting back together and remembering the proms, the pranks, and the plays. You'll enjoy reliving those memories. That history and those friends are a part of who you are. But I predict that your greatest friendships are ahead of you.

At the start, your friends will come from social situations. You'll see them in class or at the dining commons. You'll hang out together in the dorm, or be cramming with them at 3 A.M. for a test the next morning. From this context, you'll find a few friends that you'll want to know better. So, you'll intentionally spend more time together. That's how meaningful friendships begin. . .slowly, one day at a time.

You are going to have a lot in common with the people who become your closest friends, but it won't be "things" as much as it is "beliefs." You will share similar commitments in faith, character, and integrity.

But the people who become your closest friends probably won't be *exactly* like you. After all, you are one of a kind. They may wear one set of clothes the whole day, while you are more likely to change outfits three times before lunch. They may know nothing about Broadway musicals (but that won't last long if they hang around you much).

You will come to appreciate each other's similarities, and you will admire each other's differences. You will enjoy each other for the kind of person you each presently are and for the kind of person you each are trying to become.

You'll find an interesting distinction between your casual friends and your closest friends. The casual friends will be around whenever *they* need *you.* Your closest friends will be around whenever *you* need *them.*

True friendship is so much a matter of love. It comes from each of you wanting what's best for your friend more than for yourself. It is recognizing that God is working in your life through your friend, and He is using you in the same way in her life. When that type of mutual commitment exists, a bond of loyalty is forged. A paraphrase of 1 Corinthians 13:7 would say it this way:

If you love your friend, you will be loyal to her no matter what the cost. You will believe in her, and always expect the best of her, and always stand your ground in defending her.

Isn't that just the kind of friend that you want to have? I know it is the kind of friend you want to be. I'll be praying for you as you find and build these lifelong friendships.

Love, Dad

The first duty of love is to listen.

Paul Tillich

Subject: Caring
From: Dad
To: Hillary

Message: Ever since you were a little girl I've noticed something that sets you apart from most people. You have always cared about others. Now I'm not saying that everyone else out there doesn't care, because we all have some sort of regard for other people, both friends and strangers. We're considerate to those we know and we try to be courteous to people we've never met. That's all a part of being civil to one another. It's how we get along and function together.

But caring is an entirely different matter. It takes consideration to another level. Caring means being truly concerned for others. You see, my tendency is to size people up when I see them (okay, you could call it "judging"), which is wrong. I qualify them as if they have to meet some kind of standard (only I know what that standard is, of course). On the other hand, you look right past the external dimension into the heart. I don't know how you do it, but you do. You show genuine interest in others and don't prejudge them before you get to know them.

The great thing about caring is that you will always be a person others feel comfortable with. They know that you don't have some kind of hidden agenda (like me). They know you won't judge them and they know you'll listen to them.

In fact, listening may be the biggest part of caring, and this is where you really shine. You probably don't know this, but many times I'll watch you as you interact in a group. (I don't get that opportunity much anymore, but I love it when I can.) I watch as you focus on the other people, smile at them as they talk to you, and actively listen to them. Kids love you because you really pay attention to them and enter into their little worlds. And older adults always enjoy being around you because you really pay attention to them.

By caring about others in this way, you demonstrate the love of Christ to others. You imitate Him by focusing on people individually, even when you're in a crowd. I love you because you're my daughter, my flesh and blood. But I admire you and I enjoy being with you because you care about me. You enter into my world when we talk, you focus on me and laugh at my jokes. I never feel insignificant when I'm around you. Thanks for caring.

Love, Dad

It is wonderful to say the right thing at the right time.

Proverbs 15:23

Subject: Encouragement
From: Dad
To: Lindsey

Message: I had a few more thoughts since our phone conversation last night. I know you are looking for ways to be an encouragement to your friend during this tough time for her.

A little encouragement can make a big difference. It doesn't take much: maybe only a few words or a small act of kindness. It might not seem like much to you, but it could be really meaningful to her. Whenever you encourage others, you are showing that you have care and concern for them. Few things in life are so easy to give and have so much impact.

God wants her to be encouraged. You may be the way He is intending to do it. He can use your arms to embrace her. He can use your voice to speak to her.

Knowing how to be an encouragement to someone else can be tricky. Sometimes people need a word of encouragement that will challenge them. You might need to shake them up a little bit. Other times, they need a word of comfort and kindness.

The distance between a "kick in the pants" and a "pat on the back" is only a few vertebrae, but this isn't a matter of their physiology. It is a matter of your sensitivity. You have to be sensitive about *what* you say, and *when* you say it.

One final suggestion: Make sure you say and do something. Your good intentions are meaningless unless you put them into action. Don't be so worried about *how* you can encourage her that you fail to do anything at all.

Lindz, you are a good friend. I know you have her best interests at heart, and she knows that, too. Pray for God's wisdom and love, and then trust your instincts. Say and do what is in your heart. She'll be glad you did (and so will you).

Love, Dad

I fit in with them as much as I can.

Paul the Apostle (1 Corinthians 9:21)

Subject: Flexibility
From: Dad
To: Hillary

Message: Your mother often describes you as being a very relaxed person, and she's right. Rarely have I seen you get tense, even when I think you should. (I don't mean tense in a bad way; I'm talking about the good kind of tense, like before a test or a big date.) Being tense just isn't your style. You are one easygoing little puppy.

Having said that, I have noticed that on occasion you get frustrated when circumstances don't quite happen the way you want. Usually this occurs when someone else agrees to meet you at a certain time, and they don't quite make it. They're late. They keep you waiting. They lose track of time while you're watching the clock. Only then have I seen your body language begin to change—your eyes narrow, your back stiffens, and your lips tighten.

At the heart of these physical symptoms is a certain lack of flexibility, which is nothing more than adjusting to the changes in others. It's allowing for variation and movement. Flexibility is a little different than tolerance, which has more to do with letting others be themselves. Flexibility is about adjusting your schedule or your tastes to accommodate the different schedules and tastes of others.

There's an element of compromise in being flexible. It's understanding that you won't always get your way and you won't always follow your schedule—not as long as other people are involved. You may have to flex a little in order to accomplish your goal of getting someplace or getting something done.

There's another dimension to being flexible, and that's knowing which battles are worth fighting, and which ones are better left alone. Let me give you an example. Last year you had a roommate who was quite messy. Her half of the room looked like a war zone most of the time, and sometimes her piles exploded onto your side of the room. Now, since you are pretty neat, you got a little frustrated. But rather than making it a battle between you and her—thereby risking your friendship and any kind of harmony in your twelve-by-twelve-foot space—you chose to let it go. You were flexible. You didn't give up your commitment to neatness, you just didn't impose your neatness principle on her, because it wasn't worth fighting over.

Now there may be times when you must fight the battle because some principles that really matter to you are in jeopardy. These are principles of the heart, principles of integrity and self-respect. Here flexibility really isn't the issue. True flexibility means you make adjustments on the outside without compromising your inner principles.

Love, Dad

Your heavenly Father already knows all your needs,
and he will give you all you need from day to day
if you live for him and make the Kingdom of God
your primary concern. So don't worry about tomorrow.

Matthew 6:32–34

Subject: Patience

From: Dad

To: Lindsey

Message: I know you are stressing out about what is going on. I'm sorry that there is nothing I can do to help. Actually, I'm kind of glad that I can't assist you. You just have to wait to see how things turn out. This may be a new experience for you. There is actually a word for it: *patience.*

Was that too sarcastic? Well, I know you won't be offended. Let's face it. We both realize you will never be the poster girl for Patience International. You always want to know how things are going to end even before they get started. I'm not sure why you are that way. Maybe you want to avoid being surprised, or hurt, or disappointed. Maybe you are just curious. Nah, I don't think so. You are just IMPATIENT.

Impatience is wasted emotion. It is absolutely worthless. It doesn't make things happen faster or different. In fact, it is counterproductive because it distracts and upsets you.

Without meaning to preach at you (which comes easily for me), let me mention a spiritual dimension to patience. Our trust in God is reflected by our patience. On the other hand, our impatience is a matter of pride. When we are impatient, we want something to happen before God wants you to know about it. Since (or if) you are willing to trust Him with the outcome, then trust Him with the timing.

I don't want to make this a bigger deal than it needs to be. But you need to realize that impatience about the future often ruins the enjoyment of the present. If you are stressed and distressed about the uncertainty of tomorrow, you won't be able to appreciate the beauty of your circumstances today.

You have great things happening in your life right now, so

enjoy them. And you have a God who wants and knows the best for your future, so let Him handle that at His own pace.

Love, Dad

P.S. I can just imagine your prayer tonight: "Dear Lord, please give me patience, AND GIVE IT TO ME NOW!" Doesn't that seem a bit ironic?

The human body has many parts,
but the many parts make up only one body.
So it is with the body of Christ.

1 Corinthians 12:12

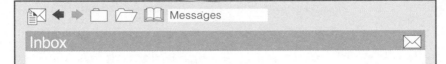

Subject: Teamwork
From: Dad
To: Hillary

Message: I'm afraid I haven't prepared you much in at least one area of life (there may be others, but I can't think of any right now), and that's teamwork. Unlike many families, we've never been big in the area of team sports. We don't watch them a lot, and you and your brother never played a lot of sports.

No doubt you have vivid memories of your one grand experience in the wide world of team sports. Remember the Blasters? That was your softball team. Who could ever forget? Softball has always been big in our town, and one of our best friends (you remember Bob) coached a team for ten- to twelve-year-old girls. I was no different than other dads; I had grandiose visions of my kids excelling in team sports. I had dreams of seeing one of my kids score the winning run and being named the Most Valuable Player.

The only problem was that you were on a team of future softball all-stars. There were girls on that team who could throw and hit a ball better than I could. At last count, four of the girls on your old Blasters team are playing college softball on full scholarships. These young ladies could play some serious ball. As for you, I think the expression "riding the pine" best described your team sport experience. You were so cute in your red and blue uniform, but your competitive spirit and athletic skills just weren't there. You entered into the "chatter" of the game while sitting in the dugout, but your conversation had more to do with boys and clothes than hitting and fielding.

After two years of softball you decided team sports weren't in your future, and that was fine with us. Only now as I look back, I wonder if I could have done more to prepare you for teamwork in the real world. Because even though your

Blasters days are long gone, you always will be on a team of some kind. Your family will always be a team—now it's me and your mom and your brother (who grew out of his He-Man pajamas, thank goodness, but never was much into team sports either). Later you will have a family team of your own.

In your chosen field of graphic design, you will more and more be involved in creative teams as you produce practical and pleasing artwork. And as a Christian, you are now and always will be part of a community of believers who—like a sports team—bring different experiences and skills and personalities to the team, otherwise known as the Body of Christ.

As you live and work together with others, learn to appreciate their unique personalities and skills. Do your best to cooperate with others so that everyone's best comes out for the good of the group. The end result will be a success and pleasing to God.

Love, Dad

But among you, those who are the greatest should take the lowest rank, and the leader should be like a servant.

Luke 22:26

Inbox

Subject: Leadership
From: Dad
To: Lindsey

Message: The person you described in your last e-mail seems like a typical authoritarian leader. That approach is not uncommon. It is used by a lot of leaders (usually the immature ones). "Do what I say because I'm in charge."

Leadership doesn't have to be that way. I'm sorry you have to endure it, but it will help you realize that there is a better approach.

I think the best leadership style (for both the leader and the followers) is "servant leadership." This is not an oxymoron. It describes the leadership style modeled by Christ. He *served* his followers; He didn't boss them around. They were motivated by what He did *for* them, not by what He threatened to do *to* them.

Authoritarian leaders are interested in making themselves look good. They want to feel important, so they often humiliate people in the process.

Servant leaders are more interested in their followers than their own reputations. They accept more than their share of the blame and less than their share of the credit. They act with humility so their followers feel important.

Right now, there is probably not much you can do to change the style of your leader. You are stuck for a while. Prayer will help, but you should pray for yourself more than for your leader. You see, you have the opportunity to exhibit leadership within your group (even though you are not "the leader"). I'm not talking about a mutiny (although that may be tempting). You can influence others in the group by the way you respond to the unreasonable demands of your leader. If you respond with a servant's heart, you'll be setting an example for the others to follow. You can change the attitude of the entire group. That is the essence of true leadership. It is not a matter of title or position or authority. It is a matter of character, humility, and service.

Love, Dad

P.S. Now, stop searching the Internet for instructions on "tar and feathering."

None are true saints except those who have
the true character of compassion and concern
to relieve the poor, indigent, and afflicted.

Jonathan Edwards

Inbox

Subject: Compassion
From: Dad
To: Hillary

Message: This is going to sound a little funny, but compassion is very popular right now. Maybe it's because we have so many reasons to be compassionate. All you have to do is read the headlines or listen to the news and you can't help but see the suffering of vast numbers of people around the world as a result of poverty, oppression, and natural disasters.

Your heart goes out to these people, and you wonder what can be done. More personally, you wonder, "What can I do?" First, let's talk about what compassion really means. Very simply, compassion is being so moved by the sorrow or hardship of another person or group of people that you want to help them. You want to give them money or personally help them with their problem. Somehow you want to get involved in the effort to improve the situation of someone who's really hurting.

There have been many shining examples throughout history of compassionate people—in your lifetime, Mother Teresa stands out—but the greatest example of all was Jesus. He not only saw the physical hurts of people, but He saw their spiritual needs as well. So He not only healed people, but He forgave their sins. Obviously we have no way of forgiving sins, and we can't heal people either. But we can offer ourselves to people in need.

You also have to realize that no matter how much compassion you show, it will never be enough. You may help one person, but there will always be someone else in need. The truth is, we will never eliminate the need to be compassionate. Jesus told His disciples, "You will always have the poor among you" (John 12:8). The natural hostility of human beings insures that wars and conflict will never cease—at least not until Jesus returns and makes the world right again.

And what about the natural disasters, like the devastating rains and floods that nearly destroyed Nicaragua and Honduras? That's where you have suffering on a large, almost incomprehensible scale. How do we deal with that? How do we explain the enormous human suffering such disasters produce? The Bible tells us that nature itself is groaning under the weight of sin in our world. That groaning literally produces natural disasters. So again, until Jesus makes the world right again, natural disasters will always be here, and they may be getting worse every year.

Where's the balance? How can you properly express compassion? My advice is that you choose one area and get involved on a consistent basis. Whether it's feeding hungry children and building shelters for the poor or providing relief after natural disasters, get involved by supporting an organization that specializes in helping disadvantaged and displaced people. You can't be all things to all people, so choose an area you feel especially compassionate about. Then match up an organization known for meeting the physical and spiritual needs of people. For example, World Vision has an excellent track record of bringing relief to people and then helping them climb out of poverty. Habitat for Humanity is another outstanding organization that builds housing for people who have demonstrated responsibility but have never had an opportunity.

You may want to volunteer your time on a regular basis. There's nothing like seeing the need firsthand, like you did when you took those trips to Mexico with your high school church group. I remember when you would return after spending Easter week in some very rural and poverty-stricken villages, you would say, "I don't know how much we're helping them, but they sure appreciate us being there." That's because you loved the people unconditionally. Remember Caesar, the little boy with the cleft palate? Someone took a picture of you holding Caesar in your lap. I'll never forget the look of joy on both of your faces.

Compassion and love seem to go together. That's why it's not unusual to have compassion for your friends and family, especially if they are hurting. Never pity people. Try not to feel sorry for others. Instead, exercise creative and constructive compassion. Without being a meddler, ask how you can help someone who's hurting emotionally. If someone you know is suffering physically, pray for that person.

Above all, let your compassion for others be motivated by your knowledge that God has been compassionate to you. Whenever you have needed God's help, He has been there for you. Sometimes you don't recognize it until after you go through your crisis, but He's always been there. And most importantly, He showed you compassion by sending Jesus to die for you, even before you knew that you needed a Savior. The Bible says that "God showed his great love for us by sending Christ to die for us while we were still sinners" (Romans 5:8). It's one thing to show love and compassion to a friend, but God loved us while we were His enemies. With God's help, that's the kind of attitude we need to have.

Love, Dad

Avoiding a fight is a mark of honor;
only fools insist on quarreling.

Proverbs 20:3

Inbox

Subject: Conflict
From: Dad
To: Hillary

Message: Oh boy, I sure don't like conflict, and I
know you don't either, but conflict is part of life (as you
found out recently). Here's my advice on conflict. First,
realize that a conflict usually originates somewhere else, so
don't take it personally. Second, rather than looking at the
differences between you and the person you're conflicting
with, look for the things you have in common. Third, if
you can't resolve your conflict, ask a third party to help you
through the issues. Finally, pray about the conflict. God is
great at resolving conflicts, as long as both parties are listening to Him.

Lessons About Your Family

I could have no greater joy than to hear that my children live in the truth.

3 John 4

Subject: Parents
From: Dad
To: Lindsey

Message: If you think being on your own is tough, you ought to try being the parent. My role as your dad has suddenly changed drastically, and I'm not sure that I like it (but I'll adjust—eventually).

I don't know whether I am being sentimental or insightful, but I'm amazed at the similarities between being a coach and being a parent.

Remember when you played T-ball years ago? I was your private coach. Every kid had a parent serving in that capacity. I stood beside you in the field (helping you face the right direction). I held the bat as you swung, and I even ran with you on the base path. Parenting in those days was very similar. You needed me (and your mom) for just about everything. I was involved in all of the decisions of your life. It was real "hands-on" parenting.

When you progressed to girls' softball, you still needed me, but my involvement was limited to the sidelines. At practice I would run hitting and fielding drills with you, and during the game I would shout instructions from the third base coach's box (giving hand signals like a mime with an overactive thyroid gland). This type of coaching was similar to how we related as father and daughter during your teenage years at home. I was still the "coach" and set the rules for curfew, and you even followed my instructions for things like school, cars, and dating. The third base coach's box was in the form of our dinner table, but those were great times as I got to "coach" you through those high school years. (Oh, you got "benched" a few times, but you never got kicked off the family team—although I did consider putting you on waivers a few times.)

You hung up your softball glove years ago (and those full-ride athletic scholarships went to the other members of the Blasters team). But as your dad, I feel a little bit like the manager of a professional baseball team. You don't need me to come on the field with you, and I'm not even in the coach's box anymore. But I'm still watching you play the game! I'm here in the dugout (which looks surprisingly like our living room), and I'm anxious to shout words of encouragement.

Sometimes it gets lonely here in the dugout, watching you from afar. But watching you play the game of life is a thrill.

Whenever you are having a bad game, give me a call between innings. I'll always be ready with a few tips. (Luckily for you, I know a little bit more about life than I did about softball.)

Love, Dad

God places the lonely in families.

Psalm 68:6

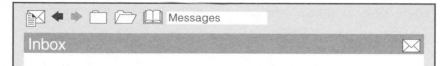

Subject: Brothers & Sisters
From: Dad
To: Hillary

Message: Next to your parents (and eventually your own kids), the blood relative you're going to be closest to throughout your life is your brother. The special bond between siblings is hard to explain. In fact, I can't explain it at all, since I'm an only child. So before I jot a few things down about you and your brother, I would like to review your other blood relationships. These may not be as important, but I think I can give you some valuable advice on how to get along with each of these groups of relatives:

Uncles and Aunts: These are generally very useful relatives because they look after you as if you were their own.

They seem to take a special interest in you because they're related to you through their own brothers and sisters, and often they see their own qualities in you (only the good qualities, of course). You are fortunate that you don't have "the uncle nobody talks about" or "the aunt who's always meddling" in your family. Perhaps that's because your uncles and aunts come only from your mother's side. Enjoy your uncles and aunts; listen to them when they give you advice and thank them when they send money.

Cousins: Your cousins come from your aunts and uncles. There's nothing like having a cousin close to your own age. I love my cousins, even the weird ones. I may not have had any brothers or sisters, but since my mom had seven and my dad four, I had a ton of cousins. Now, you have the distinction of being the oldest of seven cousins in your family, and because of that you carry a little more responsibility than I did as one of forty cousins. Can you handle the pressure? Whether you realize it or not, your little cousins look up to you in many ways, including your choice of lip gloss, clothes, cars, music, and boyfriends. So make good choices in all these areas.

Grandparents: This group of blood relatives is so important that it deserves its own e-mail (keep reading after this one). So let's go right to brothers and sisters, which is the topic of this e-mail.

I *admire* you for many things, but if there's one area where I *envy* you, it's that you have a brother. Don't get me wrong. I have never for one minute regretted being an only child, but I have a strong feeling that I would love being a brother. I would love being able to talk to someone anytime and have no pretense between us. I would love being able to know that there's someone else out there who is closer to me than anyone else because we have so much in common, even though we are two unique individuals.

That's the way I see you and your brother. You guys have a very special relationship that's hard to define. When I see the two of you together, I see two close-knit people who can laugh together, encourage one another, or simply sit quietly together and listen to music.

When you left home, I don't think your mother and I missed you as much as your brother did. He would walk into your room and just stand there, as if he expected you to somehow walk in like you used to. Of course, it didn't take him long to move all of his guitars and amps into your room, effectively converting it into his own private music studio, but I know he still thinks of it as *your* room.

Whenever you come back to visit, I think he enjoys you even more than we do (which is a lot). Your brother loves you very much, and I know you care for him deeply. Your friendships will come and go, but your brother will always be there for you, and you for him. It gives me great joy to see the love between the two of you and to know that it will continue and grow throughout your lives.

There is a famous verse in Proverbs that says, "A real

friend sticks closer than a brother" (Proverbs 18:24). I think you are fortunate that you have a real friend who is your brother.

Love, Dad

The godly are concerned
for the welfare of their animals.

Proverbs 12:10

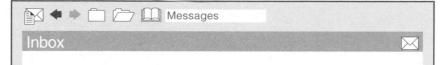

Subject: Pets
From: Dad
To: Hillary

Message: You've always loved pets. During your life
our family has had two cats, two dogs, two birds, and at
least two rodents (the cute, furry kind, if that's possible).
You also loved *stuffed* animals, although I can safely say
that doesn't include any of your pets, both dead and living.
Your room used to be filled with them. You played with
them and talked to them as if they were real. Now that
you're on your own, we've put all of your stuffed animals
into storage, but someday, when you ask for them, we'll
get them out and look at them together.

Love, Dad

Grandchildren are the crowning glory of the aged.

Proverbs 17:6

Subject: Grandparents
From: Dad
To: Hillary

Message: Have you ever seen those cute books where little kids talk about their grandparents? The kids say things like, "I like my grandma because she's squishy and she has time for me," or "My grandpa makes a funny noise when he takes his teeth out."

Grandparents have traditionally been portrayed as old people with lots of time on their hands. It's almost like a storybook, with grandparents living on farms or in Florida. At one time that was generally true, but lately things have changed.

In your lifetime grandparents are a lot younger and a

lot firmer than grandparents used to be. Most of them don't live on farms, and when they go to Florida, it's to take their grandkids to Disney World. Just look at your own grandparents. One set owned their own business (where I worked for most of my life), while your mother's parents worked for large companies. They have lived in cities, worked hard in their vocations and in their churches, traveled extensively, and have done their best to be good grandparents to you.

You can be absolutely sure that all of your grandparents have loved you like their own children. In fact, I'm told that grandparents often feel even more affection for their grandchildren than their own kids. I think it has something to do with the fact that they can love you and spoil you without having to resort to correction or discipline, which is the job of the parents.

That's one of the reasons why God is never referred to as our heavenly grandfather. Oh, people would like to think of Him that way, with a flowing white beard and a jolly laugh, like some kind of celestial Santa Claus. People want God to only be loving. They don't want His correction or discipline. But that's not God. As our heavenly Father, God is loving in a way that always wants the best for us, and sometimes that means that He will allow circumstances or other people to bring us to the point of necessary change.

Another reason why God can't be your grandfather is that the day you accepted Jesus into your heart, you became a child of God. You received all the spiritual benefits of being a daughter of God, including the inheritance of eternal life. It's an amazing thing. So, enjoy and love your grandparents and appreciate them as God's special gift to you. And thank God that He's your heavenly Father.

Love, Dad

Don't be selfish; don't live to make a good impression on others. Be humble, thinking of others as better than yourself. Don't think only about your own affairs, but be interested in others, too, and what they are doing.

Philippians 2:3–4

Inbox

Subject: Roommates
From: Dad
To: Lindsey

Message: I know you are nervous about this roommate thing, but don't be. Before God created the universe,
He knew who your roommate would be. If we can trust
Him with eternity, I suppose we should trust Him with
this part of your life as well.

Now that I've said what you already know (and what
you knew I was going to say), let me add a few other things
for you to think about. Get ready, here they come (in no
particular order other than my stream of consciousness):

Your roommate doesn't have to be your best friend.
You will have a lot in common (like the 180-square-foot

room where you live), but you aren't going to be chained to her. You will have a life outside of the dorm room.

Differences aren't bad. If you think about it, in high school everyone tried to be the same. Now that you are on your own, I think you will begin appreciating differences among people. Let it start with your roommate. Those differences will range from musical preferences to personality.

Your roommate is not a member of your family. Hey! Let's face it! We cut you a lot of slack because we love you and we have the same last name. We've got a history with you that your roommate won't have. So, show her a little more courtesy than family members usually show each other.

Respect her stuff. Don't automatically assume that she is willing to let you wear her clothes and borrow her hair dryer. Some people actually like to keep their stuff for themselves. (You wouldn't know about this, because most of the good stuff that belongs to me, Mom, or Matt has ended up in your closet, and we have forgotten that we owned it in the first place.)

Realize that some of the things that you do may irritate

her. It is hard to believe, and it isn't true as far as I am concerned, but is just possible that somehow, in some way, some other person may find a few of your cute little idiosyncrasies TO BE A REAL IRRITATION. Of course, it would be difficult for me to mention one or two (because there are so many I could choose from), but you get my drift. So anticipate what they might be; make some adjustments; and get used to a few of hers.

Learn to work out your differences. Learning to get along with your roommate is good training for marriage. I've had the same "roommate" for twenty-four years. We have to work things out because there is no way to change the room assignment.

Well, I hope those comments are helpful. I'll be praying for you.

Love, Dad

As a general rule, teachers teach more by what they are than by what they say.

Subject: Teachers & Mentors
From: Dad
To: Lindsey

Message: Thanks for asking me those questions about your classes, etc., but I don't have the answers that you need. (Wow! Did you ever think that you would hear me say that?! Please delete this e-mail after you read it because I don't want your Mom or Matt to know that I made this admission.)

As you think about a career in journalism (or any career for that matter), you need to develop mentoring relationships with people who can give you practical insights and advice. You are surrounded by a faculty and administrators who are anxious to spend time with you personally. I know that they would enjoy talking with you about your career aspirations and advising you about courses, internships, etc. But they aren't going to push themselves on you. You have to make the first move. (Hint: It is called "asking.")

Always be on the lookout for people who are doing something really well that you will be doing in the future. Maybe it is in the context of a job. Maybe it will be someone who has a really good marriage. Maybe it will be a couple who is doing a good job raising their kids. If you like what they are doing (and the way they are doing it), don't be afraid to ask for their advice. They will consider your request as a compliment.

Remember that your teachers and mentors won't have all of the answers. You'll still have to evaluate what they say. What works for them may not be appropriate for you. But think how much farther along you will be with their suggestions.

A mentor wouldn't expect you to copy him or her. You will still be free to make your own decisions (and your own mistakes). You don't have to follow their suggestions if you don't want to (like what you do with *me*).

You will enjoy having a mentor. Most people miss out on the opportunity because they are too meek to make the request. Don't let that happen to you. Take advantage of the wisdom of the people who are available to you (because you've outgrown my reservoir of wisdom).

Love, Dad

Fix your thoughts on what is true and honorable and right.
Think about things that are pure and lovely and admirable.
Think about things that are excellent and worthy of praise.

Philippians 4:8

Subject: Dating
From: Dad
To: Lindsey

Message: I know you are out on a date as I'm writing this e-mail. Now that you are reading it, the date must be over (unless the guy is really cheap and reading your e-mail is part of the date). Hope you had a great time.

I know there is a current philosophy that is critical of dating. People take it to the extreme and contend that you shouldn't date anyone except the person you are going to marry. I disagree. One of the purposes of dating is to learn about the *kind* of person you will want to marry.

However, I think there is an appropriate progression to dating. I liked the fact that your dating in high school was usually in a group. Now that you are on your own, you are going to have more occasions to go on dates alone (well, not *alone*, but with just one guy). As you spend time together, you'll get a chance to know what you have in common and what you disagree about. You'll learn if he is boring and self-centered (a typical male flaw), or whether he is thoughtful and can converse with words instead of grunts.

I know I am a relic from a bygone era. (My wing-tip shoes prove that!) And I am confused by all of the gender-equality and gender-neutral trends in society. So, I'm still opening doors for women and pulling out the chair at the restaurant table for your mom. That is how I was taught to show respect. I don't know how that translates to your generation, but don't waste your time dating a guy who doesn't show you respect and treat you as being someone special. Those other guys can be your friends, but save the dating for the guy who is more interested in you than in himself.

As dad-to-daughter, let me say that I am proud of how you are handling this whole dating thing. I am proud of your virtue and your judgment. Because you seem to have things under control, I'll start working on your brother. Matt needs help. He is still at the stage where he thinks it will impress a girl if he can burp the alphabet.

Love, Dad

He has identified us as his own by placing
the Holy Spirit in our hearts as the first installment
of everything he will give us.

2 Corinthians 1:22

Subject: Engagement
From: Dad
To: Hillary

Message: If it's only natural that a father thinks about
his daughter getting married—and it is—then it's only
natural that a father gets very anxious when he thinks
about his daughter getting married. At least I do. And not
because I don't want you to get married someday (if that's
your choice), but because I want so much for you to be
happy when you do.

I want to give you my thoughts on marriage (I highly
recommend it, by the way), but before I do I wanted to talk
a bit about engagement. I think engagement is very much

underrated. People seem to treat it like this meaningless transition period between love and marriage. You never hear couples say, "We're engaged." It's always, "We're getting married next August."

Marriage may be the goal and ultimate desire between two people in love, but I'm here to tell you that engagement is a crucial and exciting period of time that I want you to experience to its fullest. My desire is that you and your future husband see your engagement as a time to get a lot done, have a lot of fun, and grow closer together. If that happens, you will enjoy your wedding and your marriage a whole lot more.

I sound like such an expert. You would think that I've been engaged many times. Not true. I was only engaged one time, to your mother, and for only five months at that. And here's another thing. This business about couples getting engaged for a year or more is just ridiculous. It puts too much pressure on your physical relationship. I know that you are committed to wait until marriage to have sex (thank you very much), but once you get engaged, you're one step closer to marriage. It would be easy to feel that you are committed, that this is the guy you're going to marry, so why not?

There are two ways to avoid this pressure. First, keep the engagement under a year, ideally around six months. I know that won't entirely be your decision, but you can have a great deal of influence in this area. Besides, the planning of your wedding will pretty much fall to you and your mother, so you can regulate how long it's going to take. (That's the beauty of being a guy, by the way. Wedding plans seem to take care of themselves.)

The second way to stay pure during your engagement and to get everything out of the engagement period that you possibly can is to see engagement as a blessing from God. In fact, it's more than a blessing. It's a promise. I think you know that in the Bible marriage is used as a symbol for our relationship to God. As Christians, we are literally called the "bride" of Christ, and Jesus is the bridegroom (John 3:29). Someday, the bride and the bridegroom will be reunited when Jesus comes for all believers, both living and dead, so that we can live forever with God in heaven.

How do we know that's going to happen? Because of the Holy Spirit, who is God's promise. Right before He left the earth, Jesus told His disciples that they would have the Holy Spirit as a guarantee until He returned to earth again in the future. In a very real way, you are engaged to Christ, and the Holy Spirit is your engagement ring, as real as any ring you will get on your finger.

Not only does this promise of the Holy Spirit give you the assurance you need that Jesus has gone to heaven to prepare a place for you (John 14:2), but it also assures you that Jesus is coming again for you so that you will someday participate in the "wedding feast" of heaven (Revelation 19:7).

There's another benefit of this promise of the Holy Spirit (and I hope I'm not stretching things too far here). It elevates the role of engagement (when it happens) in your own life. It really is an important part of the process, so take it seriously. However, don't expect your future bridegroom to prepare a mansion for you like Jesus is for us. A cozy apartment near the beach will do quite nicely!

Love, Dad

A man leaves his father and mother
and is joined to his wife,
and the two are united into one.

Genesis 2:24

Inbox

Subject: Marriage
From: Dad
To: Hillary

Message: I think about you and marriage a lot these days, and not because I'm anxious for you to get married. Hey, I've seen *Father of the Bride* a couple of times, and I know that when that day comes I will be very emotional about letting you go. Walking you down the aisle will be one of the happiest days of my life. But I also know it will be one of the most difficult. I'm not necessarily looking forward to your wedding day because I don't know yet how I'm going to handle it.

However, when I think of marriage in general, I get very excited for you. Here's why. When I was your age—

about twenty-five years ago—I married your mother. The day was a blur, and we spent our honeymoon traveling down the coast of California (hint: Stay in one place on your honeymoon). Oh, I enjoyed the wedding and the events that surrounded it, but I *really* enjoyed setting up our own apartment. I enjoyed being our own couple, Stan and Karin Jantz. I loved your mother and I loved sharing everything with her. I loved being *married* to her. Twenty-five years later, I still do.

I remember when I was thinking about asking Mom to marry me, I was reading a bunch of books on marriage. (I always like to do a little research before making a major decision, especially when it's permanent!) One book in particular was by Dietrich Bonhoeffer, the German theologian who was executed by Hitler. It wasn't a book on marriage per se. Rather it was a collection of letters from prison, where Bonhoeffer was being held for treason. Here was this brilliant servant of God, who gave his life fighting for freedom in his country, and he took time to write some letters about marriage. He was counseling this couple about their marriage, and here is what he said: "From this point forward, it will not be your love that keeps the marriage together, but rather the marriage that keeps your love together."

Isn't that profound? What I took him to mean was that in a marriage love will come and go. I don't think he meant the principle of love, but the *feeling* of love that is so strong when you know you want to spend the rest of your life with someone. Your feelings will come and go with changing circumstances, shifting moods, and difficult times. Sometimes your feelings will change for no apparent reason. Don't be alarmed. Keep a level head, try to work through the problem, and keep the lines of communication open. Most of all, never think about giving up. Here's where the marriage becomes an incredibly important factor.

When Bonhoeffer said that your marriage would keep your love together, he was talking about commitment to each other, to your marriage, and to God. When it comes to your marriage, I pray nearly every day that you will be happy. I want you to have the joy and the growth your mother and I have had. But more than anything I pray that your marriage will become so important to both you and your husband that nothing will be able to tear it apart. Then, like your mom and I have found over the years, your marriage will not only keep your love together, but it will help it grow.

The sad thing is that in our culture—even in our Christian culture—marriage has been cheapened. Marriage has been taken off the divine pedestal where it belongs and brought down to the level of a common contract. It's no longer a sacred union ordained by God, but a quaint—and in some circles antiquated—option that becomes a revolving door for many people. People see marriage as a "fifty-fifty" proposition, where a husband and a wife create a partnership, almost like you'd put together a business. The problem is that a healthy and permanent marriage isn't built on each person going halfway. As I see it—and this is from the Bible—husbands and wives are each called by God to give 100 percent (read Ephesians).

Of course, such commitment is nearly impossible without

God. I think the only way to truly love your spouse is to love him with the selfless, "I want the best for you" kind of love that only God can produce in your life. When you commit your life and your marriage to God, you are saying to Him, "I believe everything you said." You believe that God loves marriage and hates divorce. You believe that God created marriage for our benefit and our enjoyment. And you believe that God will help both of you thrive as individuals and as "one flesh" as you love each other and glorify Him.

Wow, I've gotten kind of serious here, almost preachy. Didn't mean to. I hope you sense my passion for marriage. And I hope you know that I've been praying for you and your future husband for years. There's nothing I want more than to give you away to God's man, whoever that may be. When that day comes, you can be sure that I will be the happiest man on earth, even if I have tears in my eyes.

Love, Dad

May God, who gives this patience and encouragement, help you live in complete harmony with each other— each with the attitude of Christ Jesus toward the other.

Romans 15:5

Subject: A Husband
From: Dad
To: Lindsey

Message: Well, it is 2 A.M. I'm getting ready to pack
it in, but I wanted to send you a note before I went to
sleep. You have been on my mind more than usual these
last few weeks. I have been praying for you and your
growing relationship with "you know who." I've been feeling kind of funny about all of this. Not "ha ha" funny, and
not "something's wrong" kind of funny. But the "weird"
kind of funny that a father feels when he gets a sense that
he is losing his little girl.

It seems like just yesterday that the only other man in
your life was Mister Rogers (although you did have that

passing infatuation with both Bert and Ernie). I didn't consider Mister Rogers to be a threat to *our* relationship because I knew you could never be *really* serious about a guy in a cardigan sweater. But now you've got a new guy in your life, and he definitely is not the cardigan sweater type. (Where is Mister Rogers when I need him?)

I am not worried at all about your ability to choose a good husband. You have always been very selective with the guys you date. I know that you will immediately disqualify any guy who frequently emits bodily odors or has the name of an old girlfriend tattooed anywhere. You're looking for a guy who shares your sense of humor and integrity. Ideally, he will be a guy who considers your irritating habits to be "endearing qualities."

You know that I have been praying for your future husband since the day you were born. Without ever knowing who he would be, I wanted the Lord to be working in his life to make him the kind of man that you deserve as a husband. Maybe it is time that I told you the specific qualities I have been praying for in your future husband.

For more than two decades, I have been praying that the Lord would give you a husband who:

- Will be deeply committed to God;

- Will love you more than he loves himself;

- Will take seriously his responsibility to be a provider;

- Will respect and value your opinions;

- Will assume spiritual leadership in your home; and

- Will be a great dad to your kids by being a great husband to you.

From a dad's perspective, this is all of the important stuff. If he has the right relationship with Christ, and the right relationship with you, then everything else will take care of itself. Notice what is conspicuously absent from my prayer list:

- I don't care what he does for a living or how much he makes. So long as he is a hard worker and is committed to providing for you, then you'll do fine.

- I don't care where he lives. (Your mom may have a dissenting opinion on this one.) I would rather have you living happily across the country with the right guy than being miserable down the street with the wrong one.

- I don't even care what he looks like (but a tall guy would be nice because he could bring some height into our family gene pool).

Let me close with what your mom and I have always told you: Don't settle. Don't accept anyone who is less than God's best for you.

Well, that's enough for now. Thinking about all this stuff is tough for me. I think I'll look through your old baby photo album before I go to sleep.

Love, Dad

P.S. Don't worry. When the time comes that you decide to get married, I'll break the news to Mister Rogers.

Lessons About
Your Life

The true inner life is no strange new thing;
it is the ancient and true worship of God,
the Christian life in its beauty and in its own peculiar form.

Gerhard Tersteegen

Subject: Inner Life
From: Dad
To: Hillary

Message: The other weekend when you were home
the four of us were sitting around the dinner table comparing physical features. We've been through this before,
but it's fun to talk about the things we have in common.
I don't know about you, but it gives me a very warm
and wonderful feeling to see that my kids bear a certain
resemblance to me. I certainly wouldn't wish my peculiar-
ities on either you or your brother, but I am proud of some
similarities.

For example, we were comparing hands. Your mother
was commenting that she and Scott have similar hand

shapes. Likewise, you and I have the same kind of hands. Your shoulders are rather broad like mine, and you share my same chin. Now, those may not seem like big things to the average person, but I kind of like it that you will always have those physical traits. (I hope you don't mind.) Maybe they'll remind you of me from time to time.

The thing about physical features is that you can't do a whole lot to change them. You're more or less stuck with your hands, your shoulders, and your chin (which is a good thing . . .you'd hate to go through life without them). And even your personality will not change measurably over the years. You will always have your optimistic, loving nature, and you will always have your unique and sometimes strange sense of humor (which you also got from me). My belief is that your physical and personality features come as a package when you're born. In fact, the Bible says that you had these characteristics from the moment that you were conceived. King David wrote in a psalm to God, "You made all the delicate, inner parts of my body and knit me together in my mother's womb" (Psalm 139:13). Science today has confirmed this truth—it's called your DNA.

Okay, so you can't do a whole lot to change the basic "you," although you can work to refine and enhance your features and personality (believe me, I've done a lot of refining over the years). But there is a part of you—which I want to call the *real* you—that you can change dramatically. It's your inner life.

Stay with me for a few minutes. I don't think we've talked about this before, and honestly I didn't come to realize how important my inner life was until I was much older than you. So it's not unusual that you haven't thought about this very much. But if you catch even a portion of what I'm going to tell you, I think you'll start a journey that will take you to some places of great spiritual depth and personal growth.

Gordon MacDonald first made me aware of the importance of cultivating your inner life in his book, *Ordering Your Private World*. I use the word "cultivate" very deliberately, because that's the word he chose in the book. According to

MacDonald, your inner life is like a garden. When you culti-vate a garden—that is, when you prepare the soil, kill the weeds, plant the seeds, and water the plants and flowers—you are doing everything you can to help it grow. And chances are you're going to have a lovely garden. On the other hand, if you simply scatter a few seeds around and then neglect your gar-den, you may get some plants and flowers, but they'll likely be scrawny. Worse, you'll have a crop of weeds that will all but choke and destroy the fledgling plants.

I think you can easily make the comparison between the garden and your inner life. It is possible—and I highly advise this—to cultivate your inner life. Prepare your heart through prayer to receive the good things God has for you. This doesn't mean everything you take in has to be religious. Technically, everything in the world belongs to God. However, there's a lot of corruption out there, so you have to be selective about what you let through the gateways of your ears and eyes, because it goes from there into your mind and heart, which make up your inner life.

Be selective about what you read, watch, and listen to. I'm not trying to lecture to you here, because you are on your own, and I can't dictate these things for you. I don't even want to tell you what to do, at least in a specific sense. You are fully capable—and you are fully responsible—to make these decisions for yourself. All I can tell you is that what goes into your mind and heart comes out in your life. (I've learned this from experience.)

The other thing I've learned from experience is that I am the most content and I have the most inner peace when my inner life is in order. When I carefully cultivate my own garden, I have a much clearer path to God, and my relationships with others are more meaningful. Believe me, it isn't easy, and the struggle to cultivate never ends. But with God's help and your own discipline, you will experience the satisfaction of a private world that is both ordered and productive.

Love, Dad

Don't let anyone think less of you because you are young.
Be an example to all believers in what you teach,
in the way you live, in your love, your faith, and your purity.

1 Timothy 4:12

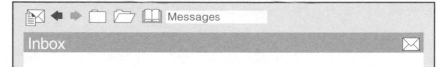

Inbox

Subject: Goals
From: Dad
To: Lindsey

Message: I am in the middle of setting my goals for the new year. I wondered if you were doing the same thing (since you are more goal-oriented than the third monkey running up the ramp to Noah's ark).

I don't think we ever discussed the "do's and don'ts" of goal setting. (You were probably busy talking on the telephone when I tried to discuss this subject with you during the last few years.)

You may want to set goals for all aspects of your life: spiritual, mental, social, financial, physical, etc. Knowing where you want to go is important, but you've got to know how to get started. Here are a few guidelines that might help.

- Your goals should be in writing. Keeping them in your head isn't very effective. You need to put them on paper so you can review them.

- Your goals should be specific and measurable. Set a goal that lets you check your progress. For instance, "wanting to know God better," is admirable, but it is not a well-defined goal. A better-stated goal might be to read through the New Testament during the year, or to have a daily prayer time.

- Your goals should be ambitiously obtainable. If you make them too easy, then they will be meaningless. If you make them impossible to obtain, then they will be discouraging.

onyourown.com

- Your goals should be accompanied by an action plan. Suppose I have a goal to lose ten pounds (okay, fifteen); I've got to have a strategy for doing it (exercising more often than once a millennium).

- Your goals should be renewed. Check your progress periodically to see how you are doing. You may have to adjust the action plan to keep on course.

Don't worry. You won't be tested on this e-mail. But I am curious to hear about your goals for the year. Talk to you soon.

Love, Dad

And we know that God causes everything to work together for the good of those who love God and are called according to his purpose for them.

Romans 8:28

Subject: Problem Solving
From: Dad
To: Hillary

Message: No matter how hard you work to achieve your goals, you will invariably run into challenges along the way. Despite your best efforts to get along with people, there will always be those who conflict with you in some way. Just when you think you are closest to God, temptation will rise up and meet you head-on.

I'm not trying to be negative, just realistic. Life is full of problems. So the question you have to ask is not, "How do I avoid problems?" Rather the question should be, "How do I solve them?" Allow me to give it my best shot.

If you run into challenges in the pursuit of a goal,

about the best advice I can give you is to *persevere*. The other day your brother was trying to build a cooling system for his computer so it could run at a faster (and therefore hotter) clock speed. He had these parts scattered all over the place. There were little rubber hoses with a pump and a container of water (I'm not kidding), and he kept at it, trying to figure out a way to cool his computer. The first two systems he designed failed, and I could see he was getting a little discouraged, so I told him the old Thomas Edison story. You've heard this before. After working for months on the light bulb, Edison was asked why he kept at it after failing so many times. The inventor replied that he hadn't failed at all, but rather had discovered hundreds of ways *not* to do it. Now Scott was only up to two tries, but I told him that he hadn't failed, but had merely discovered two ways *not* to build his cooling system. I encouraged him to keep at it, to persevere.

I want to tell you the same thing. When things go wrong on a project, when the art isn't coming the way you want it, hang in there. Be persistent. Make the necessary corrections. Persevere.

If you run into problems with people, perseverance isn't as important as *preparation*. In other words, study human nature. Get to know people and how they tick. I know you took that basic psychology class last year, and you loved it. I remember taking the same class when I was in college, and it truly gave me insights into human nature (including my own). As you get to know people, especially their likes and dislikes, you can relate to them better, thereby avoiding certain conflicts.

Finally, when it comes to temptation and the ultimate result that temporarily breaks your fellowship with God (it's called sin), my best advice is to *pray*. First of all, pray that God will help keep you from temptation (I think that's in the Lord's Prayer). When temptation does come, pray for strength to avoid caving in. And if you do cave in, pray and ask God to forgive you, effectively eliminating all kinds of problems down the road.

Persevere, prepare, pray. Not a bad way to go. I think I'll try those myself!

Love, Dad

Be strong and courageous, and do the work.
Don't be afraid or discouraged by the size of the task,
for the LORD God, my God, is with you.
He will not fail you or forsake you.

1 Chronicles 28:20

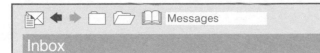
Inbox ✉

Subject: Success
From: Dad
To: Lindsey

Message: I am happy for you that you got the internship position. You are definitely building a good resume.

You are on a real winning streak, so now is a good time
to remind you of something important: While Mom and
I are impressed with your accomplishments, we are proud
of you for the kind of person you are. The distinction is
significant.

Did you ever notice how we have congratulated you
over the years? Whenever you received an award, we said
we were *excited* for you, but we never said we were *proud*
because you won the award. We were always proud of you

for the hard work that it took to win the award, but we would have been proud of you whether or not you received the prize.

Many people make the mistake of defining success by their accomplishments, or their awards, or their bank balance. Don't ever define success by such terms. Instead, view "success" as the journey that you take on the way to reaching your goals. Success is not the destination; it is the daily progress you make in small steps toward the destination. "Success" is the hard work that propels you in the direction of your worthwhile goal.

Lindz, you certainly have no problem being motivated for achievement. But I want you to enjoy a sense of satisfaction as you work diligently on a daily basis to achieve your goals. If you are growing closer to God, that is success. If you are becoming more prepared for your career, that is success. If you are developing strong friendships, that is success. These are worthwhile goals, so the pursuit of them is success in itself.

We are impressed and excited about your internship—

that's an accomplishment. But even more, we are proud of who you are and who you are becoming—that's success.

Love, Dad

Many of life's failures are people who did not realize how close they were to success when they gave up.

Subject: Failure
From: Dad
To: Lindsey

Message: I can't remember the last time I had to console you because you failed at something. I know it is a new experience for you, so think about this: You are not a failure simply because your attempt was unsuccessful. You're only a failure if you refuse the attempt because it may not succeed. The greatest failure is the failure to try.

Lindz, you tried! You should be proud that you did. I am.

Love, Dad

Whatever you do,
you must do all for the glory of God.

1 Corinthians 10:31

Subject: Career
From: Dad
To: Hillary

Message: One of the proudest moments of my life
was the day you left for college. Actually, we went with
you on the day you left for college, because someone had
to haul all of your stuff (your mother and I gladly volun-
teered). We checked you into your dorm room, met your
roommate, made sure everything was in order, and then
came to the moment of good-bye. We stood together in
your room, said a prayer, and then Mom and I got back
into our car and drove home, leaving you behind.

I was proud on several levels, first of all because you
made the decision to venture out. I hope you never got the

impression that we were trying to get rid of you, but we did encourage you to leave home for school, especially since you had chosen to attend a Christian university. We were confident that you would grow in every dimension of your life—mentally, emotionally, and spiritually (so far so good). I was also proud of you because you boldly ventured into a major field of study, which is kind of unusual for a freshman. You decided to study art, specifically graphic design.

I've got to be honest with you. Before you left home for college, I wasn't sure that you would graduate with a specific career in mind. I can't say I was bothered by this prospect. After all, I graduated from college with a degree in English literature, which isn't exactly the kind of major that propels you into a career-type job. As it turns out, I didn't really "use" my major in my retail business career, although it has come in handy as I've been writing more. So had you decided to major in some kind of liberal arts field, I would have been perfectly happy, knowing that somewhere along the line you would use your knowledge or experience.

As it is, you've decided to study a field that offers some wonderful career opportunities. You've also chosen something that suits your artistic sensibilities very well. Since you were a toddler, you have been comfortable with a paintbrush in your hand (and we have the pictures to prove it). You didn't go much for sports or music lessons, but you took painting lessons for eight years. And now you're learning all about art and graphics and computer applications, and in a couple of years you'll be ready to take your skills into the marketplace. Before you know it you'll be ready to launch into a career.

So what does that mean, anyway? What's a career, and why is it so important? First of all, as a woman (boy, that sounds strange) you are living at a great time as far as developing a career is concerned. The opportunities for women to enter into a quality career have never been better. As a woman you are living at the best time in history to choose a profession, get an education, get the necessary training, and succeed.

I have no doubt that you will succeed in your graphic design career. Even if you decide to do something else with your major, I know you will do well. That doesn't mean you won't have challenges. Every career and every job comes with its share of frustrations, setbacks, and inequities. Don't look for them, but don't be surprised when they come. The thing that will surprise you is how difficult it is to maintain balance in your life when you're in the middle of building a career. Here's what I'm talking about:

I understand you well enough to know that building a career is not your top priority in life. It's something you want to do, but it isn't an obsession. It isn't your dream. If I read you correctly, I believe that your overall dream and desire is to finish college and begin a career; build a life with your future husband; share your happiness with him and the family the two of you will have together; and honor God in everything you do, whether it's your career, your family, or your individual life.

Maybe I'm projecting my own dreams onto you, but I don't think so. Not for a minute would I claim to know what's best for you in these critical issues of life, and I would never want to assume that this is the only course your life should take. Only God knows what's best for you, and only He knows how your life is going to unfold. I believe the choices you will make in the next few years are yours, but I would advise you to make those choices with the help of God. Seek Him in all you do. Read His Word daily. Pray and ask God for guidance. Take advice from people who are growing in Christ. If you faithfully do these things and trust God for the results, you can confidently make your choices and know that you are going to succeed—maybe not precisely in the way you planned, but in the way God desires for you. If I could summarize my thoughts on this matter, I probably couldn't do better than Psalm 37:4 : "Take delight in the LORD, and he will give you your heart's desires."

Love, Dad

I have learned how to get along happily whether I have
much or little. I know how to live on almost nothing or
with everything. I have learned the secret of living
in every situation, whether it is with a full stomach
or empty, with plenty or little. For I can do everything
with the help of Christ who gives me the strength I need.

Philippians 4:11–13

Subject: Money
From: Dad
To: Lindsey

Message: So, this is a momentous day! May I have a
drumroll, please: You now have your own credit card! It
came in the mail today. I opened the envelope. I couldn't
help myself. The card looks so beautiful—especially the
part that has your name embossed on it (instead of mine).

Up until now, the rule for using *my* credit card has
been easy to follow: You can use it only in an emergency
(and I specifically told you that a cute sweater on sale at
the mall was *not* an emergency).

But now, you've got your own card and you are going
to have to establish your own rules for how you use it. As

you might expect, I have a suggestion for two rules that you may want to adopt. Here they are:

Rule 1: *Never charge anything on the credit card unless you have the cash in the bank to pay for it.* I hear you asking, "So what good is the credit card then? Why don't I just write a check instead?" That is exactly the point. The credit card is just for convenience. It may be easier to charge something instead of paying cash or writing a check (like buying gas at the pump). But don't get in the habit of using the credit card as a bank loan. Otherwise, you will be going further into debt with every charge.

Rule 2: *Always pay off the credit card bill in full every month.* This will be easy to do if you follow Rule #1. It will be tempting to pay only the "minimum monthly payment" amount. The credit card company always makes it look so small. But resist the temptation.

Why do I tell you all of this? Because now you have the ability to go into debt. This is dangerous because you need to learn to live within your income. It is all a matter of having a good sense of direction: If your income exceeds your outgo, then your upkeep is going to be your downfall. Cute, but true.

So, let me know if you want me to mail your new card to you, or whether you just want to pick it up the next time you come home. Congratulations! This is a rite of passage.

Love, Dad

P.S. When you come home, we will have a little ceremony when you take the scissors and cut up *my* credit card that you have been using. Hey, why wait? Do it now! But call me, because I want to hear the "snip, snip" over the phone. It will be music to my ears!

W e must look on all things of this world
as none of ours, and not desire them.

Clement of Rome

Inbox

Subject: Stuff

From: Dad

To: Hillary

Message: Thinking about all of the stuff we've been
helping you move around since you went on your own has
prompted me to think about, well, *stuff.* When you were
little, you loved stuffed animals, so whenever a birthday or
Christmas or any special occasion came around, we
bought you at least one little creature. Soon all of your
friends figured out that you liked stuffed animals, so they
did the same thing. Before you hit three years old you had
an impressive collection of Peter Rabbit animals (your
favorite), Disney characters (Tigger was your prize), and
an odd assortment of winsome creatures, including

Mr. Pickle and Mr. Hotdog.

Then, at a certain point in your life, you started collecting other stuff, most notably clothes and shoes. By the way, Mom was going through your closet the other day and found a large collection of shoes with humongous soles. (I think you only wear a size 5 shoe, don't you?) These shoes Mom found had five-inch soles made of rubber or wood. No wonder you're the tallest five-foot-two-inch person I know.

In addition to the personal stuff you've been accumulating, Mom has been collecting stuff *for* you, like our old dining room set and some dishes we aren't using anymore (Mom figures you'll use them in your first apartment or house), some linens, the old futon from your room (just exactly what is a futon, anyway?), and the usual array of lamps nobody wants. Of course, even though this stuff, which used to be our stuff, is now your stuff, we get to store it for you.

In fact, I just paid the bill for a storage facility near your school. I had no idea it cost so much to rent a five-by-eight-foot crate. I guess the price included those two burly mover guys who picked up the aforementioned furniture and dishes and linens we brought to the apartment you rented last summer. The burly mover guys took it to an undisclosed location, jammed it into the five-by-eight-foot crate, and stacked it on top of some other crates, no doubt rented by other fathers for daughters with lots of stuff.

So now here you are at the tender age of twenty-one, and already you have more stuff than entire nations used to have back in the Middle Ages. You have stuff in your dorm room, you have stuff here at home, and you have stuff in a storage facility. And you're just beginning life on your own! What's going to happen when you get into your career, move into your own place, eventually get married, buy a house, and have a family? What are you going to do with all your stuff?

Well, I'll let you figure out your storage needs, but I would like to comment on the stuff itself. First of all, allow me to define what stuff is in the first place. Essentially, stuff is material. Whether we're talking about stuffed animals, clothing, jewelry, electronics, cars, furniture, or even houses, it has all been made or manufactured from raw materials. Depending on the design and the quality, some of these things can be very beautiful, so beautiful that we think they enhance us or give us prestige. Other things can be highly functional and useful to our lives, so that we wonder how we ever got along without them. And still other things are of no value to other people, but they have great sentimental value to us, because they remind us of certain important people or events.

When things fall into the category of beautiful, functional, or sentimental, it's very easy to get attached to them. So attached that we lose perspective and think that we would never be the same without them. It's okay to value certain things, but remember that things, no matter how valuable, can be lost, stolen, or destroyed. By the same token, things can be replaced.

What can't be replaced are people and relationships. This may sound a little trite, and it may fall into the category of "Yeah, I knew that, Dad," but I want to say this, because I see too many people, too many couples, and too many families living under the control of material things. They work hard so they can have nice things, but then the nice things take charge of their lives, so that they're working *for* the things. The last thing I want for you is to be caught up in an endless cycle of payments and interest charges as you pay for all your stuff. I don't want you to experience the stress and worry associated with such a condition.

And even if you are fortunate enough to never have to worry about money, the accumulation of wealth can be just as big a problem as the lack of wealth. Materialism in any form, whether you have a lot or a little, can interfere with your relationships, especially your relationship to God.

To keep your life in perspective, keep all your stuff in perspective.

Love, Dad

Where there is simplicity, there is no artificiality.

Albert E. Day

Inbox

Subject: Simplicity
From: Dad
To: Hillary

Message: A few simple ideas on simplicity as it relates to your life:

- It's better to have a few things you highly value
  than a lot of things you don't care that much about.
- If you haven't worn something in a year, give it
  away.
- You can't attain simplicity unless you eliminate
  clutter.
- When you give God the "first" of everything—your
  time, your money, and your attention—life becomes
  much simpler and you become more effective.

It isn't your position that makes you happy or unhappy.
It's your *disposition*.

Subject: Perspective
From: Dad
To: Lindsey

Message: Two bricklayers were working on the Notre Dame project in Paris in the twelfth century. A bystander asked: "What are you doing?" The first man said: "What does it look like? I'm laying bricks." The second man said: "I'm building a beautiful cathedral."

In the midst of all your hard work, keep your perspective. You aren't just going to class, working a job, and studying for tests. These are important bricks in the cathedral of your life.

Love, Dad

Don't let the excitement of youth cause you to forget your Creator. Honor him in your youth before you grow old.

Ecclesiastes 12:1

Subject: Leaving Home
From: Dad
To: Hillary

Message: I just read a statistic in the newspaper. It said that 70 percent of the kids who leave their state for college don't return home after graduation. Well, you left home for college, but you didn't leave the state, so I guess the jury is still out on whether you will ever come back. We'd love to have you around after you finish school, of course, but we know there's a good chance that you're on your own for good. Your mom and I knew there was a chance you would not return home when we sent you off. We just didn't know the reality would set in quite so soon.

The generous prosper and are satisfied;
those who refresh others will themselves be refreshed.

Proverbs 11:25

Subject: Generosity
From: Dad
To: Hillary

Message: No matter how much or how little you will
have throughout your life, always be generous. Generosity
doesn't come from pity or from obligation. Rather, a generous spirit comes from a heart that is overflowing from gratitude. Some people are afraid to be generous because they
think it means they won't have enough left for themselves.
This is utterly backwards. God Himself asks that we give this
idea of generosity a try, first to Him and then to others. "Try
it!" God says about giving him our offerings. "Let me prove
it to you! Your crops will be abundant" (Malachi 3:10–11). I
think God is telling us that He will bless us in ways we
haven't even thought of—if we will only be generous.

If I had my time again, I would be stronger
on social injustices and less involved
in parties and politics.

Billy Graham

Subject: Politics & Worldview
From: Dad
To: Hillary

Message: Your mother should be writing this e-mail, because she is the one person in our family who is passionate about politics. Where most women swoon over handsome actors, Mom loves to watch the news analysts on TV. Mom gets so involved in the political process that she talks back to the television when she disagrees with a politician or a commentator.

You are probably more like me than your mother in the area of politics. You are interested but you don't get too worked up when someone with an opposing view grabs the microphone. I know you have some definite political convictions, but you aren't a campaigner. You don't feel compelled to convince others that your political point of view is the right one (pun intended).

That's not to say that you shouldn't campaign about *something*. As you know, I strongly believe that each person has a worldview of one kind or another, and that only one worldview is correct. I remember when you took that class as a freshman, "Foundations of Christian Thought." You came home at Christmas break with the syllabus from the class and excitedly showed me its contents. Your class was all about understanding why the Christian worldview is the only viable one, particularly as it relates to the truth about God, our world, and ourselves. You discovered that the two other primary worldviews, humanism and pantheism, leave the one true God out of the picture completely.

I think you're going to find that certain political views follow certain worldviews. You may not find a complete correlation between a particular political view and a particular worldview, but often the similarities will be striking. That's why I would encourage you to continue studying your own Christian worldview. Learn for yourself what the Bible says about our responsibility to the government and to our fellow citizens. Find out what the Bible says about the sanctity of life and the need to care for the disadvantaged. Don't get me wrong. The Bible is not a political book; in fact, it's remarkable how far the Bible seems to stay from politics. Rather, the Bible is a manual for life, because it was written by the One who created all things and who knows us better than anyone else. The Bible tells us how to relate to God (love Him with all of our heart, soul, mind, and strength) and to others (love our neighbor as much as we love ourselves).

So even if you ever develop a keen interest in *politics,* never forget about *people.* They're an important part of your world and your worldview.

Love, Dad

Lessons About
Your God

Remember the days of long ago;
think about the generations past.
Ask your father and he will inform you.

Deuteronomy 32:7

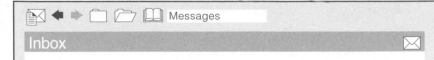
Subject: Your Past
From: Dad
To: Hillary

Message: Today is Thanksgiving, one of my favorite holidays. Mom and I are at the cabin. Scott is driving over this morning from home, others are arriving in a couple of hours, and you are flying up from school even as I'm writing this e-mail. So you won't read this until you get back to your room on Sunday night. You can't imagine how excited I am to see you today and the whole weekend, along with the entire family. We're not a big family, but with your grandparents and cousins and aunts and uncles around, we'll have a warm and wonderful time.

I know you love family time during major holidays, especially now that you're on your own. You love the sights, the smells, the sounds, and the memories all of that creates. You love the warm feeling you get when you curl up on the couch. You love playing board games with your cousins. You love going to the movies (I think we're going to see one tomorrow). You love laughing and making others laugh.

I've been reflecting on family this morning, especially your heritage. Like most people in America, you aren't that far removed from immigrant families who came across the Atlantic in this century. We can't trace our ancestry to the Pilgrims, of course, but you do have some exciting and meaningful events in your past. Your great-grandfather on my side, for example, came with his brother from Russia when he was fifteen (this was right before the revolution) and settled in Canada. Your great-great-grandparents on your mother's side came from Sweden and settled in Minnesota. Your grandparents on my side were born in Canada, but somehow ended up in California. Mom's grandparents found their way to Oakland, where both your grandparents were born (that means that on your mom's side you are third-generation Californian, which is kind of unusual).

When you think about your ancestors, how they ventured out on their own and moved—not from one town to another, but from one continent to another at a time when travel was just a little more difficult than it is today—you've got to admire their spirit and determination. They were seeking more opportunities, a better life, and in the case of my grand-father, freedom from oppression and poverty.

I know that you clearly remember when the four of us traveled to Germany a few years ago to visit the descendents of my grandfather's brothers and sisters—the ones he left behind in Russia. When the iron curtain dropped, families whose roots were in Germany (like my grandfather's) were allowed to return. Among those who found their way to Germany were these blood relatives of yours, whose fathers and mothers and grandfathers and grandmothers had not ventured out. Consequently they were trapped in a Communist nation for seventy-five years. Like me, I'm sure you will never forget that afternoon when several of these dear family members told us harrowing stories (through a translator) of tragedy and survival. They didn't mean to be dramatic; it was their story.

Another part of their story—the biggest part—was their faith. I was deeply moved when I realized that these immigrants knew the same hymns I remember my aunts and uncles and grandparents singing when I was growing up. They were hymns that expressed a deep and abiding faith in God. This is your heritage, too, because that same faith strengthened your ancestors on both sides. It has been passed down to you through at least four generations, yet at every level each of us has had to embrace that faith individually. Even though you have the privilege of a Christian ancestry, you had to make the personal decision to accept Christ into your life (remember, God has no grandchildren). When you have children someday, it will be your privilege to tell them the Good News about

Jesus, but it will be up to them to receive it.

In one sense you are a product of your past, but in another and even more important respect, what you do and the decisions you make affect your future.

Love, Dad

But those who wait on the LORD will find new strength.
They will fly high on wings like eagles.
They will run and not grow weary.
They will walk and not faint.

Isaiah 40:31

Subject: Faith
From: Dad
To: Lindsey

Message: Mom told me that you called today. She says that you are worrying about your future. (What a surprise.) You have a lot of things going on in your life, and it is natural that you are curious about the direction the Lord will lead you. But don't let anxiety overtake you.

This is a matter of your faith in God. Not faith in the sense of whether you believe in Him (because you do). Not faith in the sense of whether you will stay committed to Him (because you will). But faith in the sense of whether you can trust Him. Whether you trust His direction. Whether you trust His timing.

Psalm 23 says that the Lord is your Shepherd. Look at what this means:

- He is *not* your chauffeur. He doesn't take you wherever you tell Him you want to go.
- And He is *not* your tour guide. He doesn't tell you in advance where you will be going and what you will be doing.
- He is your Shepherd. The Shepherd leads the sheep where they need to go to be fed and pro-tected. He knows what is best for them.

Having faith in God is more than a belief in His exis-tence. It is turning control of your life over to Him. I know that is what you want to do. But if you are stressing out about the future, then you are holding back on God a little bit. True faith means that you can relax with His timing and direction. I don't think sheep have a very high anxiety level. They seem content to let the shepherd be in charge.

I know exactly where you are in this process. You are thinking: "I am willing to go wherever and whenever He leads me. I just want to know *now* how it is going to turn out in the future." Well, Lindz, it's not likely that the Lord is going to tell you in advance. He wants you to learn to trust Him. That is what faith is all about.

How do I happen to have such keen insight into your struggles? Well, I struggle with the same thing (notice that I use the present tense). I'm always anxious to see the next page on God's outline for my life. Tell you what. I'll pray for you if you pray for me.

Love, Dad

P.S. Actually, I'll pray for you whether or not you pray for me. It's a dad thing.

Without wavering, let us hold tightly
to the hope we say we have,
for God can be trusted to keep his promise.

Hebrews 10:23

Inbox

Subject: Hope
From: Dad
To: Hillary

Message: Have you ever thought about some of
the amazing things that have been developed for popular use in your lifetime? And how about some of the
incredible events that have occurred since you came into
the world on that cold and foggy December morning?
Let's see, you were born in 1977. Here's a short list of
some products *which did not exist* before then (or at least
they weren't available to the general public):

1. Personal computers
2. Compact discs

3. The Internet
4. Home-delivered pizza
5. Fax machines
6. Starbucks coffee
7. Cellular telephones
8. DVD
9. Seinfeld

And here are just three momentous events which have occurred *during* your lifetime (I'm sure you can think of more):

1. The breakup of the Soviet Union and the fall of the iron curtain
2. The development of a common currency in Europe
3. The original *Star Wars* trilogy and the release of the first film in the *next Star Wars* trilogy

And there's one more event in your lifetime, which is so rare that it has only happened once since the birth of Christ. This is what you will tell your grandchildren someday: *I was there for the new millennium.* Can you imagine? In the prime of your life, at the point when you are finishing school and starting a career, you are smack dab in the middle of the greatest calendar event in, well, one thousand years. Not only that, but you are living in the time of greatest change the world has ever known. I suppose people in every era have believed they were living in the time of greatest change, but it's never been truer than now. Technology continues to race along at a breakneck pace so that only your brother and a few other super-techies know what's going on. Social changes seem more dramatic now than they were when I was growing up (and I grew up in the sixties). And the shifting world political scene is simply amazing.

Because change is happening so rapidly, people are understandably nervous. I don't mean hand-wringing nervous (although there is plenty of that going around), but more like a general anxiety that comes from uncertainty. Whenever you live around a lot of change—whether it's on the job, in school, in your family, or in the world—you feel insecure about the future. You wonder what's going to happen. Will I be able to get a job? If I get a job, will I have job security? Will I get married, and if I do, how do I know the person I marry will be right for me? Will I have a happy marriage? Will we be able to afford a house? Will we feel safe? Will there ever be peace in my community. . .in our country. . .in the world?

I've been thinking about this over the last few months, especially with the advent of the new millennium. And I've come to the conclusion that the things people are looking for—prosperity, security, happiness—can really be summed up in one word: *hope*. People are hoping against hope that everything will go well with their lives. Some people take more measures to prepare for the future than others, but everyone hopes the future will be better. This includes the foreseeable future, which are the months and years ahead, as well as the distant future, which is the time beyond your life and mine.

I can't give you any guarantees about the foreseeable future, except that it's going to be exciting because it's going to change. You just don't know what's going to happen. However, I can give you a big guarantee about the distant future, which begins when your earthly life ends and eternal life kicks into gear. This is when you realize "the hope that is within you," which is God's guarantee that you will spend eternity with Him, as long as you have made peace with God through Jesus Christ.

Knowing that you have done that gives me hope! I know that our relationship on earth, as good as it is, is only temporary. Someday when this old world is through and we are all together in heaven, we will fully become all that God wants us to be, and we'll be able to see that in each other. I really believe that. Meanwhile, you have your life ahead of you. God has some wonderful things for you to do, including giving hope to others. When you meet someone with no hope, remember that only Jesus can give him or her the hope they need. And you may be the person God uses to give it to them.

Love never gives up, never loses faith, is always hopeful, and endures through every circumstance.

1 Corinthians 13:7

Subject: Love
From: Dad
To: Lindsey

Message: Thanks for the Father's Day card. Your enclosed note was really special. It made me cry (which you know is not an uncommon occurrence on subjects of this kind).

I want to be a good father because I love you and Matt. And part of being a good husband includes being a good father. These things are obvious (hopefully).

But I also want to be a good father so I can teach you about God. You have a heavenly Father who loves you even more than I do (if that is possible). I realize that your perceptions of your heavenly Father's love are influenced

by your earthly father's love. I hope you sense that my love for
you is:

Unending. I have loved you ever since you were born,
and I will love you as long as I live. God's love is actually better. He loved you *before* you were born, and will
love you for the rest of eternity. I can't compete with
that.

Unconditional. I love you no matter what. Now, there
have been times when you put me to the test on this
one. But my disappointment about your behavior (in
those rare instances) never broke my love for you.
This is the amazing thing about God's grace. His
love is unrelated to what we do (or don't do). There
is nothing you can do that would make Him love
you more. And there is nothing you can do that
would make Him love you less.

Unbelievable. You and I have always had a great love for each other. But it has gone through stages. It has gotten deeper over the years. While your progression from diapers to diploma seems like a blur, we have two decades of building a relationship with each other. Each year our relationship strengthens. The same is true of God, only more so. The more you know about Him, the more amazed you will be by Him. His love for you is incredible. It is incomprehensible.

Thanks again for your kind and thoughtful Father's Day sentiments. I can't love you as much as God does, but no earthly father could love you more than I do.

Love, Dad

P.S. to God: Thanks, Lord, that I have a daughter who loves her dad. Not every father has that privilege.

Grace is love that cares and stoops and rescues.

John Stott

Subject: Grace
From: Dad
To: Hillary

Message: Every time we all get together for a week-end or a family gathering of some sort, I find myself thanking God for His grace to our family. When I do that, I'm basically thanking God for being so good to us. There are so many different paths our family could have taken. There are so many other choices you and your brother could have made. There are so many bad decisions your mother and I could have made. But for some reason we made the right choices, and at least to this point in our collective lives, we are on the right path. And I think I know the reason why.

God has been gracious to us. All you have to do is look around at other families and other people who aren't doing as well. I don't want to compare ourselves to others, but it's hard not to see that many other people we know—and millions we don't know—are really struggling with life. They face unbelievable challenges and seemingly insurmountable odds. And when I hear about another person or family buried beneath a heavy load of despair, or I read about a family crushed by the anxiety of an illness, I can only thank God for His graciousness to us.

I remember you once told me about a friend of yours who chalked up such goodness to "luck." He said that if you have good health or work in a job you liked or even found a prime parking space, then you were lucky. Well, I'll give him the parking space, but I really don't believe that the other major things in our lives come about by pure luck. I believe that God is very much involved in the details of our lives, and that He directs us and answers our prayers and graciously gives us the things we need because He loves us, not because we deserve them.

So what about the families who pray and trust God and

yet face difficulties? Is God gracious to them as well? Absolutely. God's grace doesn't operate on some sort of sliding scale, whereby some of us get more grace than others. The simple fact that we are alive and have some measure of joy in our lives means that God is gracious. Remember that because of sin, we deserve to die. But God has given us life to enjoy, even in the middle of difficulties. Even those people who turn their backs on God have life and can enjoy much of what it has to offer.

By no means is the life of our family finished. By the grace of God, we have many years to go. And it's possible—in fact, it's almost guaranteed—that we are going to face difficult times. But we will get through them as we have in the past, and we will find God's goodness and faithfulness in the middle of our challenges. That's what the grace of God is all about.

Love, Dad

He [the Lord] has removed our rebellious acts
as far away from us as the east is from the west.

Psalm 103:12

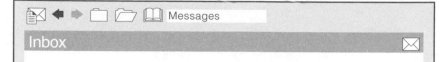

Subject: Forgiveness
From: Dad
To: Lindsey

Message: I had a deep thought when I was having devotions this morning. I'll share it with you (just in case you don't have time for your own devotions today).

Our sins don't surprise God. He knew all about them even before we were born. I should believe that God's forgiveness is complete since He sent Christ to die on the cross for my sins, knowing in advance what those sins would be.

That's it. I didn't say it was a long thought, just a deep one. Cogitate on it for a while, and then let me know what you think.

Love, Dad

Fear of the LORD is the beginning of wisdom.
Knowledge of the Holy One results in understanding.

Proverbs 9:10

Subject: Knowing God
From: Dad
To: Hillary

Message: Do you have a personal statement of purpose? I've never mentioned this before, so I wouldn't be surprised if you don't. In fact, most people haven't even thought about coming up with a statement of purpose for themselves. I didn't develop one until I was at least thirty (that seems like such a long time ago). I remember being challenged in a seminar of some kind to do on a personal level what most organizations do on a corporate level: Write a mission statement or a statement of purpose. The idea is that when you have something written down that defines who you are and what it is you want to get done, you will be more successful.

When I ran our Christian bookstore, I took our executive staff through the process of writing a mission statement for the company. It wasn't as easy as it sounds. For one thing, you don't want it to sound too commercial, and you don't want the statement to be too trite. And when you add the fact that we were selling Bibles and Christian books and such, we had a tricky balance to maintain. Honestly, I forget exactly what our mission statement was, but I know that it contained these three elements: glorify God, serve the customer, and make a profit. As for my own personal mission statement, it goes something like this:

The purpose of my life is to know God, to glorify God, and to influence others to do the same.

What do you think? It's pretty simple, but I can tell you that those few words have motivated and directed me in ways I can't even measure. Because I've had some direction and purpose, I haven't wandered aimlessly, wondering what I should do. Don't get me wrong. I have done different things and I've wandered a little, but for the most part my various jobs and activities have all related to my single purpose, so that at this point in my life, I am on the path I want to be. I'm not as far along as I'd like to be, but I'm heading in the right direction, and I believe I'm fulfilling (at least in part) my personal statement of purpose.

If you were to ask me for help in constructing your own statement of purpose, I would tell you that there's one thing you need to have at the heart of your statement. No matter what else you include, I believe that this must come first in terms of being a lifelong pursuit: get to know God better. If you make this a priority for the rest of your life, everything else you do will fall into place. That doesn't mean you will automatically be a success in the world's eyes, but you will be successful in the eyes of God.

Here's what happens when you get to know God better. As you get to know Him, you will love Him more, because you will appreciate more and more who God is and what He wants for you. I would even put *knowing* God above *loving* God in terms of your everyday activities and long-term goals. I'm not saying that knowing God is more important than loving God, because Jesus Himself said that the most important thing we can do in our relationship to God is to love Him. However, I believe that it's impossible to love God unless you know Him. Even after you become a Christian, you don't have this natural desire to really love God. You may have a heart of gratitude for what God did for you, but even that spirit of love is impossible without *knowing* what it is God did for you. That's part of the salvation process.

Knowing God involves more than just knowing about God. It's one thing—and it's a good thing—to know that God is holy and all-powerful and all-knowing and eternal and infinite and all that. But you also need to know *how* God has operated in human history, what His desire is for you now, and what His plans are for the future (most of that can be found in the Bible). It's also incredibly rewarding to find out how God has worked in the lives and through the lives of other people to accomplish His purposes, because there's a 100 percent chance that He wants to work in you and through you to do something very special.

As you get to know God a little more each day, your life will take on more meaning and you will feel more fulfilled. Because as you get to know God better, you will get to know yourself better.

Oh, and if you happen to come up with a statement of purpose, e-mail it to me. I'd love to read it.

Love, Dad

$\mathbf{Y}$ou know these things—now do them!
That is the path of blessing.

Jesus Christ (John 13:17)

Inbox

Subject: Believing God
From: Dad
To: Hillary

Message: You're going to find out throughout your life that most people believe in God. In fact, I just read a statistic in a magazine that something like 96 percent of all people in America believe in God. That figure astounded me until I read the article which accompanied the statistic. That incredible percentage includes many different religions—such as Hinduism, Islam, Judaism, Mormonism, and Christianity—all of which claim to believe in God. And then there are those who don't claim to belong to any particular religion, but still believe there's a God out there.

So who's right? I mean, whose God is the real one? Or does everyone believe in the same God? Are we all climbing up the same mountain on different trails, destined to reach the same single peak where we will all see the same God? These may sound like silly questions, but millions of people who say they believe in God believe that this is the way it goes. And they back up their reasoning by saying that a God of love would never condemn anyone to hell (by the way, the same magazine survey said that 72 percent of all people believe in heaven, while only 56 percent believe in hell). Therefore we're all going to make it to heaven, or at least those who try to live good lives will make it.

There are times when this reasoning is hard to refute, because even though we've taught you about God and I know you've personally accepted the God of the Bible, it's hard to discount the beliefs of others, especially when they seem so sincere. Well, like I said, you're going to encounter a lot of people who will say they believe in God, but they will refuse to accept your "narrow" definition of who God is and what He expects of us.

As my favorite theologian, R.C. Sproul, once said, there's a difference between believing *in* God and *believing* God. Simply believing that there is one God doesn't mean that you are going to do what He says. The Bible says that even the demons believe in God (James 2:19), and *they* certainly don't do what God says. On the other hand, when you *believe* God, you believe what He says and take His words to heart. When Jesus, who is God in the flesh, said "no one can come to the Father except through me" (John 14:6), He meant it. There isn't any way back to God—there isn't another way to gain God's favor and secure your eternal destiny with God—except through the person and work of Jesus Christ.

People want to believe in God, but they don't want to believe Him. They don't want to do what He says. Remember this when someone calls your beliefs "narrow." There aren't many ways to God. Only one. And I thank God that you've chosen that way. You really believe God.

Love, Dad

Trust in the LORD will all your heart;
do not depend on your own understanding.
Seek his will in all you do,
and he will direct your paths.

Proverbs 3:5–6

Subject: God's Will
From: Dad
To: Lindsey

Message: Your last e-mail was theologically deep.
I'm thrilled that you are grappling with the questions of
how God wants to use you. I'm just not sure that I can
give you a clear answer (because I'm still grappling on my
own). Anyway, here goes. . .

You asked: "How can I know God's will for my life?"
Here's my answer: "I don't know." But I do have a few
thoughts about it that might be helpful to you.

God's will isn't like the game where you guess which
of the three shells is hiding the bean. God doesn't hide

His will and then furiously move it around to confuse you. But many people mistakenly believe that God's will always involves a guessing game. They think that God has a preferred "Plan A," and if you choose wrong you will be stuck with an inferior "Plan B" for the rest of your life.

Be encouraged by this thought: Before He created the universe, God knew the choices you would make in your lifetime. In His sovereignty, He can arrange the circumstances of your life as He wants them to coincide with the choices you will make. So, you can be faced with a lot of choices, and they could all be acceptable in the context of God's will. (I hope this relieves your pressure of worrying about choosing the "one right" college, so you will have the "one right" career, in which you will meet the " one right" guy to marry, to have the "right" kids. If that were the case, then one person getting off track could throw the whole world out of sync.)

onyourown.com

Your own talents and interests can give you a clue to God's will. He probably wants you to use the skills and abilities He has already given to you. Look at your own life. He gave you a natural talent for writing. You are so creative with your essays and stories and articles. So, I get the sense that He will somehow have you using your writing abilities. On the other hand, I don't think He will be asking you to do anything in the medical field since you usually barf and faint at the sight of a hypodermic needle.

There is a momentum to God's will. You probably won't find Him asking you to do something totally different than what He has prepared you to do. He builds on our past experiences to take us to the next step.

God wants us to find joy and fulfillment in what we do for Him. So, don't think that following His will requires that you be unhappy or uncomfortable. He's not going to lead you into a situation that will make you miserable. To put it in terms relevant to you. . .God won't call you to be a missionary in Siberia just for the sheer torture of making you live without a blow dryer or a clothing store. That doesn't mean that you can always determine God's will by choosing the option that is most appealing to you. (Otherwise, all of the missionaries and pastors would be in places like Santa Barbara or Hawaii. Somebody has to get stuck with Fresno.) But God knows what you need and what is best for you. He has got the perfect situation in mind for you. You might not recognize it at first, but trust Him:

> *"For I know the plans I have for you," says the*
> *LORD. "They are plans for good and not for disaster,*
> *to give you a future and a hope."*
>
> (Jeremiah 29:11)

Prayer plays a big part in knowing God's will. Remember

onyourown.com

that prayer includes both talking to God and *listening* to Him. Now, I don't expect that you will actually hear a James Earl Jones-type voice booming down from heaven. But when you enter into God's presence in prayer, He can guide your thoughts. That is all a part of knowing His will.

Here is a radical thought: All that you need to know about God's will is in the Bible. Many people waste a lot of time trying to determine God's will over the insignificant details of life. I personally don't think God cares whether you choose cereal or pancakes for breakfast, and you certainly won't find a Bible verse about it. But the Bible tells us what is important to God, so those things ought to be our guidelines for His will. Jesus summed it up this way: You are to love God with all your heart, all your soul, and all your mind, and you are to love your neighbor as yourself (Matthew 22:37–39). There it is! That is God's will for you (and the rest of us).

I know what you're thinking: "It can't be as simple as that." But it is. When you boil it all down, God's will is not so much a thing, a time, a place, or a person. Instead, it is the attitude of your heart. If you are actively involved in loving Him and obeying Him, then you are doing what He desires. If we are focused on Him instead of ourselves, then God will take charge of leading us, and we just need to go with the flow. But don't just take my word for it. God has specifically promised you that He will be responsible for guiding you if you obediently depend upon Him:

> *"Trust in the Lord with all your heart; do not depend on your own understanding. Seek his will in all you do, and he will direct your paths."*
> (Proverbs 3:5–6)

Well, that's the end of my sermon. Don't stay up too late

tonight analyzing God's will about whether you should do your homework or what you should wear tomorrow. (The answers are "yes" and "clothes.")

Love, Dad

"For I know the plans I have for you," says the LORD. "They are plans for good and not for disaster, to give you a future and a hope."

Jeremiah 29:11

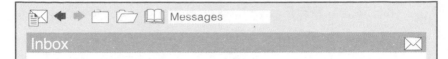

Inbox

Subject: Your Future
From: Dad
To: Lindsey

Message: Sorry that I haven't written for a few days.
I have been buried at work. And I have been trying to figure out how to answer your question about your future.

I know that you are struggling with the "What are you
going to be when you grow up?" question. You said you are
envious of your friends who seem to know exactly what
they are going to do in the future. I'm glad for them, but
don't feel too bad if you don't have an answer for yourself
yet. For most people, their career path is determined by
the first job they get after college. So don't sweat that
question yet. Resist the pressure to decide right now. You

have your whole life ahead of you, and most people change career paths several times. Just keep working hard at your studies, and explore the possibilities.

Let me give you a suggestion. Don't think so much about *what* you will do in the future. Instead, concentrate on *who* you will be in the future. What you end up *doing* is not as important as who you end up *being*. It's not what kind of job you have that matters; it's the kind of person you are that counts.

Do you remember your first job? If you don't count the occasional baby-sitting gigs, it was reshelving the files in my law office. (That was in the days before you knew about the minimum wage law.) Remember how I told you that each probate file represented someone's life? When life is over, all of a person's fame and fortune can be reduced to a file folder in some lawyer's office (that some third grader is going to put on the file room shelf after school). But there is something that can't be placed in the probate lawyer's file. . .the quality of a person's character.

onyourown.com

The prospects for your future career are promising. You have had great summer jobs at the television station and the ad agency. Your articles in the newspaper are always impressive. If journalism is the field you choose, then I have no doubt that you will succeed.

But your probability for career success is not why I'm excited about your future. I really don't care if you end up *writing* for a newspaper or *delivering* them. What excites me (and your mom) are the qualities we see in you: your enthusiasm for life, your kindness and sensitivity, your integrity, your virtue, and most importantly, your love of God.

I still have that picture of you and your brother hanging in my office. You know—the one with your goofy expressions with the inscription that reads:

> *I have no greater joy than to hear that my*
> *children are walking in the truth.*
>
> (see 3 John 4 NIV)

You must be about nine years old in that picture. More than a decade has passed. The glasses have been replaced by contacts. The pigtails and the braces are gone. The little girl is now a woman. Despite all of these changes, my hope for your future remains the same. . .that you keep walking with the Lord and living in His truth.

Love, Dad

ALL ABOUT BRUCE & STAN

Bruce Bickel spent three weeks as an aspiring actor before spending twenty years as a perspiring attorney. While he has abandoned his stand-up comedy routines, Bruce brings a lively and humorous style to his writing and speaking. He lives in Fresno, California, with his wife, Cheryl, and their son, Matt. Their daughter, Lindsey, resides at Westmont College, about 250 miles from home. Bruce and Cheryl are the co-chairs of the Parents Council and Bruce is on the Board of Trustees at Westmont College.

Stan Jantz has been involved in Christian retailing for twenty-five years. He serves as the public relations manager for Berean Christian Stores. Stan lives in Fresno, California, with his wife, Karin, and their son, Scott. Their daughter, Hillary, resides at Biola University, about 250 miles away from home. Stan and Karin serve as the co-chairs of the Parents Council at Biola University.

Bruce & Stan have collaborated on eleven books, with more than one million copies in print. Their passion is to present biblical truth in a clear, concise, correct, and casual manner which encourages people to connect in a meaningful way with the living God.

The authors welcome your comments. Contact them at:

P.O. Box 25565, Fresno, CA 93729-5565

OR

E-mail address: guide@bruceandstan.com

Be sure to check out the Bruce & Stan website at:

www.bruceandstan.com